Writing While Parenting

Writing *While* PARENTING

BY

Ben Berman

ABLE MUSE PRESS

Able Muse Press

www.ablemusepress.com

Library of Congress Cataloging-in-Publication Data

Names: Berman, Ben, 1976- author.
Title: Writing While Parenting : essays / Ben Berman.
Description: San Jose, CA : Able Muse Press, 2022. | Includes bibliographical
 references and index.
Identifiers: LCCN 2021060271 (print) | LCCN 2021060272 (ebook)| ISBN
 9781773491110 (paperback) | ISBN 9781773491127 (ebook)
Subjects: LCSH: Berman, Ben, 1976- | Authorship. | Parenting. | LCGFT: Essays.
Classification: LCC PS3602.E7583 W75 2022 (print) | LCC PS3602.E7583
 (ebook) | DDC 814/.6--dc23/eng/20220301
LC record available at https://lccn.loc.gov/2021060271
LC ebook record available at https://lccn.loc.gov/2021060272

Printed in the United States of America

Cover image: *Circling Words* by Alexander Pepple
 (with *Ring1* and *Ring2* by Yan Krukov)

Cover & book design by Alexander Pepple

Earlier drafts of many of these essays were written for *Grub Street*, *A Fine Parent*, *Mass Poetry*, *Solstice Literary Magazine*, the *Sagamore*, and *Teachers & Writers Magazine*.

Able Muse Press is an imprint of *Able Muse: A Review of Poetry, Prose & Art*—at www.ablemuse.com

Able Muse Press
467 Saratoga Avenue #602
San Jose, CA 95129

For Sadie and Noa,

the best little metaphors

a father could ever ask for

CONTENTS

Writing While Parenting

Writing While Parenting

The Right Frame

O N THE SAME DAY that my older daughter was born, my grandmother died.

This has always felt like perfect material for a poem, a poem that, unfortunately, I've never figured out how to write.

At first, I thought it might lend itself to a meditation on liminality and what it means to navigate birth and death at the same time, or perhaps some sort of musing on the deep but elusive spiritual connection between two souls who would never meet.

However, the problem with those approaches was that they were primarily driven by abstract ideas and didn't evoke the intense, emotional experience of those dizzying weeks.

So I started over and set out to write about the unsettling sense of dislocation I felt upon folding baby blankets while thinking of shrouds and the unbridled enthusiasm that overtook me at my grandmother's funeral when I saw distant cousins and shared my good news.

But it felt irresponsible to write about my daughter's birth in such a morbid and neurotic way.

I wondered if I was trying to make sense of something that resisted sense, so I attempted something a bit more lyric, focused on what it was like to talk to my grandmother on the phone as she was dying—each of us in separate hospitals on opposite sides of the same state—and how I held my newborn on my chest as I listened to my grandmother's final labored breaths.

I wanted the poem to pivot on the word *labor*, but there was too much backstory and context to convey for the weight of that moment to register.

So I decided to zoom out and approach this more thematically, thinking about how funerals often evoke competing and complicated emotions.

That unleashed a flood of memories—the elderly man with severe dementia who groped my wife just after her mother's funeral, my great-aunt slapping me across the face for crying when my grandfather died. Not to mention all those funerals from my Peace Corps days that involved butchering goats and shoveling graves.

But the poem was getting too big now, too shapeless.

I tried bringing it back to the present moment, reflecting on how for years I'd spoken to my grandmother every evening at six o'clock, a ritual always featuring the exact same questions, and now suddenly there was just this void.

But *void* was too strong a word. Lost in the joy, exhaustion, and sudden onslaught of domestic duties, on most days I barely even registered my grandmother's death as an *absence*.

I wondered, then, if I was the wrong narrator, and decided to write the piece in the voice of my father, who held his newborn granddaughter in the morning and then drove an hour west to hold his mother's hand as she died.

But it was too personal a story to play around with perspective, so I quickly switched to writing about narrative distance itself and how a single story changes depending on the lens.

It only took me a couple of lines to realize that this approach was way too meta.

I couldn't tell by now if the problem was that I didn't have an angle or if I had too many. All I knew was that I couldn't do anything—with material that felt like it should write itself.

Every morning, I'd sit down to write and would look at the pictures on my desk—my grandmother on one side and my daughter on the other—wishing there was some magical way to connect them, knowing that I was in it for the long haul now and would just have to wait until I found the right frame.

What Writing Feels Like

I T'S BEEN over a year since my wife and I last went out to dinner. But it's our anniversary, we have a babysitter and a gift certificate, and even though we are both suffering from sleep deprivation we are doing our best not to yawn.

We promised each other that we wouldn't talk about work or the kids, but it can be hard to find other topics to discuss when you spend every waking hour either at work or with the kids.

And to tell the truth, we're a little bit out of practice: it's been a few weeks since we last had a conversation that didn't involve dishes or diapers or crossing an item off one of our to-do lists.

Still, it's nice to hold hands across the table even if we're speaking in spurts. I tell her about some book I've been reading; she tells me a story about one of her students.

Maybe it's the wine, or maybe it just takes a little time to shed the dailiness of our lives, but my wife mentions something about how she used to go rock climbing nearby and how she thinks that the Outward Bound trips that she went on in her twenties were some of the most formative experiences of her life—how they made her dig deep into herself to do things that she didn't think she could do and how those small moments of resiliency and courage have stayed with her for all these years.

I start telling her about this Gary Snyder poem that I used to love back in college and how I never understood why a poem about *the power within* would be titled "Without" until I joined the Peace

Corps and suddenly found myself *without* friends or family, *without* electricity or running water, *without* any other choice but to rely on an inner strength I didn't think I had.

We start talking about whether you can love something before you understand it, and when the waiter places our entrées in front of us, I barely even notice because I am looking at my wife, not just looking at her but seeing her, remembering how it felt when I first fell in love with her and would look at her ankles and think, *Those are the loveliest ankles that I have ever seen.*

Soon we're discussing whether we'll stay in our condo forever or maybe one day move somewhere that feels more like us—with a yard and a creek in the back.

I tell her about this idea I have for a grant that would offer me more time to write, and she tells me that she would love to spend the summer leading students on ropes courses. We're talking about work, I guess, but really we're talking about identity, about our pasts and our future.

We've somehow finished our dinners, but when the waiter drops off the check, we're not ready to go home. So we walk past the car and head on over to the brand-new grocery store on the other side of the lot.

It will be an adventure, we tell each other.

But it doesn't take long before we are shopping for what we need, checking unit costs, and trying to remember whether we have enough snacks for the rest of the week.

Whatever we had is gone.

The word *Express* flashes in front of us, and we think not about the feelings deep inside our souls but about the most efficient way out of the store.

But it doesn't matter. For a brief while, we felt so free to flirt with possibilities, and when we walk back into the cold and the wind starts slapping at our necks, we feel not numb but alive.

Poets vs. Writers

I AM SITTING all alone at the bar when a woman approaches me. She has short, platinum-blonde hair with tight bangs and is wearing bright pink lipstick. She is at least six inches taller than I and is probably ten years younger.

Hello, she says.

Hello, I say.

I'm Ingrid, she says, extending her hand.

Ben, I say, shaking it.

Normally, I would have no idea what to say next, but since we are at a writers' conference, I ask, *What do you write?*

Fiction, she says.

I'm used to poetry conferences and am still figuring out how to hold conversations with authors who write books that other people willingly read, so I simply say, *Any particular kind of fiction?*

Fantasy, she says. And then, *High fantasy.*

I'm not sure of the difference between fantasy and high fantasy and don't want to offend her by asking some question about evil overlords or shape-shifting nymphs if those aren't things that high fantasy writers write about. So instead, I just nod my head and say, *Wow,* and take another sip of my beer.

What do you write? she asks.

Poetry, I say.

Any particular kind of poetry? she asks.

Contemporary, I say.

Now it's her turn to nod her head and say, *Wow*, and I'm not sure how to explain that that was just a joke—that any poem recently written is contemporary—so instead, I decide to double down on my attempt at humor and say, *High contemporary*, hoping that this will clarify that I am actually a very funny person.

But she just nods her head a little more vigorously and tells me that she's never met a poet before. And maybe I'm just slightly insecure about my size, but suddenly, I have this brief moment of paranoia that Ingrid is only talking to me as research for her novel and that there is a good chance I am going to end up as a character in her chapter about wood elves.

I check to make sure that she is not staring at my ears, then quickly try to steer the conversation back toward her. *What's your fantasy novel about?* I ask.

She tells me that she's only 550 pages in and doesn't want to talk about it until she's further along.

What are your poems about? she asks me.

I already know now is not the time to explain that poems aren't really about anything—that to paraphrase what a poem is about is to ruin the experience of the poem—so instead, I simply describe the piece that I was working on this morning, which involved (but was not about) the very first time I found a fully formed poop in my older daughter's diaper and was so excited that I called my wife over and asked her to take a picture so that we could send it to her uncle.

Ingrid is no longer nodding her head vigorously. In fact, Ingrid looks disgusted.

And it occurs to me that, unless you are a new parent or a dog owner, you might not be used to talking about the various textures of poop in such a casual manner, so I try to explain that

I was using the occasion of my daughter's first fully formed bowel movement to meditate on the importance of, well, form.

Ingrid asks me if I am messing with her. I tell her that, no, I am not messing with her, that earlier—when I made the comment about high contemporary—I was just kidding around, but that the poem about my daughter's poop was actually the very poem that I was working on this morning.

I am about to explain that it is a part of a sequence written entirely in terza rima, which is this form of interlocking rhyming tercets, when Ingrid smiles and tells me that she has to get something from the coatroom and wishes me best of luck with my poetry.

I return to sipping my beer, and as I look around the room— at all these gregarious fiction writers who look so impossibly comfortable in their own skin—I can't help but wonder what it would feel like to be a novelist rather than a poet.

In fact, I already have an idea for my first story—about a pixie from the Amazon who meets some sort of elfish elder that has emerged from Middle-earth to share the wisdom of his ancient band of poets.

Writing *Tips*

Maybe it's a Jewish thing—the result of God making us snip our members if we want to be members of the tribe—but I always get a little nervous when students start asking me for tips.

Don't get me wrong. Some of the most common tips are worth repeating: *Show, don't tell*; *get rid of adverbs*; *avoid clichés*.

But whenever I attempt to throw out some straightforward advice, my suggestions always seem to wobble, turn out less like perfect spirals than tipped passes up for grabs.

Hemingway suggests that a story ought to resemble the tip of an iceberg and claim some of that submerged gravitas—the glance on its way to becoming a glimpse, the deep vision emerging from a limited view.

I love explaining Hemingway's theory to my students, but his approach has never worked for me. My icebergs always turn out too slippery. At best, they slant two ways at the same time—like so many of my favorite words.

Tip, for example, can mean both *to furnish* and *to remove*.

Recently, while conferencing with a student, I offered her the oldest tip in the book: *Write what you know.*

And yet, ever since my daughters were born, and I developed an ever-persistent case of daddy brain, it's not knowing that interests me but the feeling of almost knowing—the constant sensation of a word on the tip of the tongue—*the gap that is intensely active,* as William James writes, that ephemeral *sense of our closeness.*

My First Book Interviews
My Second Book

Strange Borderlands: It is an honor to finally meet you, and I really appreciate your taking the time to respond to my questions.

Figuring in the Figure: It's truly my pleasure.

SB: To begin, I was wondering whether you would consider yourself more of a sequel or a betrayal.

FitF: Well, let's just say that every second-born child grows up in a slightly different family than the older sibling. Sometimes, we want to follow in your footsteps, and sometimes we want to be everything that you're not. There have been many studies looking at how birth order affects personality, and even creativity, but don't forget that *betrayal* and *tradition* come from the same Latin root.

SB: *Follow in my footsteps?* I was filled with stories about political upheavals in the developing world; you cough up small lyric meditations on changing diapers in the middle of the night.

FitF: I like to think of it as a policy shift: you were interested in foreign affairs, I'm focused on domestic ones.

SB: But why resist the political? We're living in an age where people are starting to celebrate cultural isolation. Who needs more small poems with small epiphanies?

FitF: There is nothing more important than taking the time to think deeply about how we understand the world. We live in a world of fake news. Reading and writing poetry offers us an opportunity to probe all the ways that we've been misinformed, sometimes by our own minds.

Keats writes about *the capability of being in uncertainties*, and poetry asks us to willingly trouble what we think we know, to reconsider our sacred truths on a regular basis. I long for the day when every incumbent campaigns for reform.

SB: *Reform?* How is a book written entirely in terza rima—a form invented seven hundred years ago—a nod toward *reform*?

FitF: One of the things that drew me to terza rima is that the form—with its intertwined rhyme scheme—seemed to serve as a counterpoint to all the disconnects of modern life.

Don't get me wrong, fractures are an essential part of poetry—we write in broken lines. But *the poem*, as A.R. Ammons writes, *is an existence which can incorporate contradictions, inconsistencies, explanations, and counter-explanations and still remain whole.* There is great overlap in travel, poetry, and parenting in terms of how they complicate our narratives.

It reminds me of that quote often attributed to John Wilmot—*Before I got married I had six theories about bringing up children; now I have six children and no theories.*

SB: But isn't writing about one's kids bound to be sentimental?

FitF: No more so than poems about travel.

Don't forget, you were filled with sensational material—poems about eating termites and falling into quicksand. You had to navigate your way past all the reductive narratives in order to discover your submerged and layered truths.

But you had the freedom to inhabit the world of a foreigner. You could poke holes in all the old narratives of your youth—allow those experiences of being a stranger in a strange land to upend whatever you thought you knew.

It's different when you're a parent. You suddenly feel this responsibility to construct a narrative about the world for your children, to offer them a center that just might hold.

And going back to your question, there's a difference between writing poems about your children and writing poems about the transformative, humbling, and perplexing experiences of becoming a parent. There is great creative energy in the collisions between who we are as people and who we are as parents. The danger is to think of it as a merging.

I think that's what drew me to writing in rhyme and playing with figures of speech—all those collisions of meanings within words.

SB: Don't you ever worry that all that wordplay will amount, at best, to the embarrassing, chummy humor of dads?

FitF: There's always that groaning danger with puns, especially if nothing's at stake.

But I tried to think of it as an opportunity to explore transformations—how *furry* can turn into *fury*, how *refrain* can become *foreign*. I was interested in an almost kabbalistic sense of interconnection and paradox.

Parenting does strange things to you emotionally. It breaks you down in every way. We fall helplessly in love with these helpless little things. It is exhausting and deeply vulnerable work. But there are times when exhaustion gives way to exhilaration, when *weakened* sounds almost like *awakened*.

A Body of Writing

SLEEP DEPRIVATION does strange things to a body.

For months, my one-year-old had been teething and rarely made it more than a few hours without crying for our attention, while my three-year-old had gotten into the habit of climbing into our bed in the middle of the night, wedging her way between us, kicking off all the covers, then asking for milk.

I have never needed a whole lot of sleep, but there was something about the constant disruptions throughout the night that made writing the next morning nearly impossible.

Most days I would rise early, make my way to my desk, open my journal to a new page, and realize that my mind was as blank as the paper in front of me. I would attempt to locate some choice phrase only to discover that the word bank in my head was operating on bankers' hours. At best, by my third cup of coffee, I could get myself into the kind of trance where I could record some clumsy dance of thoughts and dreams. But rarely could I concentrate deeply enough to shape that material into a poem.

I think it was because I had given up on maintaining a regular writing routine that I signed up to join a newly formed *Hevra Kadisha*—a group of *holy friends* who, in the Jewish tradition, are responsible for attending to the dead. About once a month or so I'd join a small group of men at the funeral home to help clean and prepare the *met*, or deceased, for burial.

And although it seems counterintuitive, even though I now had less time to write, I suddenly found myself writing more.

Often, I would return home from *Tahara*—the process of ritually washing the deceased—and simply feel the need to record the experience: the faint but sterile smell of antiseptic soap, the gaunt mortuary tools, the loose and pale skin that would tear so easily, the bright blood oozing out of open wounds, the gauze as white as glue, all the men singing comforting melodies as we cleaned and dressed the body.

But more than that, there was something surreal about my evening routines—how I would go from pouring water all over my one-year-old as she squirmed in the tub to pouring water over the body of the deceased a few hours later, from lifting the cold and stiff back of the *met* to cuddling into the warm and tender skin of my wife—and journaling offered me a way to make sense of those unsettling parallels and contradictions.

Writing, then, began to feel holy, if we think of holiness as a state of heightened attention, awareness, and compassion.

And yet I didn't want to write, or at least publish, poems about *Tahara*. I worried that it would cheapen the experience. *Tahara* brought me to a place of great humility, and I didn't want my ego to take over by thinking about it as creative material. Instead, I wanted to find a way to let these tensions play out without writing directly about them.

I soon found myself writing what would become my third book, *Then Again,* a collection of short prose narratives in which each piece opens with a single-word title and then develops by exploring various meanings of the title word. After writing about twenty of these, I realized that I could eventually connect each title to the next—*Breaks* to *Tears, Tears* to *Openings, Openings* to *Spots*—and my goal became to create a giant word loop until the titles traveled all the way back to the beginning.

This created an interesting opportunity, because even though the title words were closely related, the stories bounced back and forth between very different phases of my life: in one, I'd be slaughtering a goat in rural Zimbabwe; in the next, I'd be lying on a hammock with my one-year-old fast asleep on my chest.

Soon, much like my life, the collection began to feel like both a wildly disjointed collage and a perfectly intricate puzzle.

But writing, for me, requires just the right amount of existential angst. And it was just as I started to get back into a writing groove that I drove down to the funeral home after putting my girls to sleep and learned that the deceased that evening was a young man, about half my age. He didn't look dead. He looked like one of my students. He looked as though he should have been napping on the beach.

I came home afterward and couldn't sleep. I did not feel holy. I felt gaping holes of faith. I felt the need to be close to my daughters and ended up sleeping on the floor of their room just so I could hear them breathing.

And when I woke up a few hours later and made my way to my desk to figure out the next word in the loop, it no longer felt like just a puzzle. I was desperately trying to see the book's form as its body, not just its shape or structure but form as a living thing, a body with a soul.

Writing *Then Again* became my way of embodying disconnects in a form that stressed deep interconnections, of trying to reconcile the irreconcilable by tending to the complex worlds hidden inside words.

Brain Storms

A GOOD POET, WRITES Randall Jarrell, *is someone who manages, in a lifetime of standing out in thunderstorms, to be struck by lightning five or six times.*

Maybe it's this year's harsh winter, or maybe it's just the never-ending flurry of activity in my house, but lately, the creative process has felt less like standing in thunderstorms and more like trudging through deep snow, desperately trying to clear a path.

Like writing, there's something romantic about shoveling fresh snow—that is, until the wind slaps your neck, and your fingertips begin to burn.

Then, it's work, and it feels like work.

And anyone who has ever breezed their way to the end of a draft knows the feeling of effortlessly clearing a path through sidewalks and driveways only to find a barrier—made entirely of plowed snow and chunks of ice—between themselves and the open road.

It is dense and dirty, and there is nowhere to put it, and it's always just when you're about to start chipping away at it that you remember your elderly neighbors down the street.

By the time you get back from shoveling their path, fresh snow has turned your sidewalk into a blank page.

Your next-door neighbor is waltzing up and down their driveway with their brand-new snowblower, shooting perfect arcs into their yard.

But just as you lift your fist to the skies to curse the gods for assigning you Khione, minor goddess of snow, as your muse, you see your one-year-old looking out the window with absolute marvel and awe.

She is clapping and shrieking, and you suddenly see the world through her eyes.

The sky is falling. There are clumps of crystals everywhere. And all this work almost begins to feel like play.

Dancing like Superb
Birds-of-Paradise

Because I am always trying to secretly train my three-year-old to become a writer one day, I am very selective about which games we play.

Hide-and-seek shares some common ground with poetry—writing, after all, is a process of discovery—but there are only a few good hiding spots in our condo and my three-year-old's approach to hiding reminds me of those confessional poets who always reveal a little too much.

Charades, too, has potential given that it was originally a game of literary riddles. But neither my daughter nor I is a particularly skilled actor, and both of us tend to just jump around the room with a roll of paper towels on our heads saying, *Rhymes with municorn.*

Red light, green light has too clear a goal, too straight a path.

However, there is something about Mother may I, our game of choice as of late, that feels similar to writing with its balance of structure and freedom, its constraints that free the imagination, and its narrative framework that reminds us that stories are ultimately driven by the relationship between a character's goals and the obstacles in the way.

After all, my three-year-old's aim is to get from one side of the room to the other, and when I tell her, *No, you may not take six turtle steps forward; you must crabwalk sideways into the wall,* it provides just enough conflict and tension, the perfect amount of falling action before her climactic dive for my feet.

But writing is as much about process as it is about craft, and secretly training a child to become a writer involves so much more than simply exposing them to the intricacies of plot development.

You also have to encourage their natural love of open-ended play, and Mother may I's true appeal involves the challenge of making up new and ridiculous ways to move about the carpet: *flopping like an otter, jumping over the moon like a cow.*

And after all those Sisyphean afternoons of watching my daughter with her crate of toys—dump and fill, dump and fill— what an absolute joy it is to play with her in such imaginative ways.

May I take three princess steps forward? she asks in her sweetest voice.

No, I say. *You may run in place like a hamster, you may chase your tail like an overexcited puppy, you may hover over by that lamp like a moth.*

And we keep playing and inventing until it's late, and we're both tired, until I can finally convince her that it's time to brush her teeth and hibernate like a bear.

Zen and the Art of Poetry

WE ARE DRIVING up to New Hampshire for a winter weekend getaway and are halfway up the mountain when big heavy flakes of snow start to fall out of nowhere. My three-year-old notices how tightly I am gripping the wheel and clenching my jaw and starts asking over and over: *Are we here yet? Are we here yet? Are we here yet?*

Poems, for me, often begin with such tiny slips of language, and there is something about her substitution of *here* for *there* that feels riddled with angst, as though she is posing some sort of Buddhist *koan* about the ever-elusive here and now.

Not yet, I say, although the truth is that this might be about as present as I ever get, attentive to the stop-and-go of traffic, to the give-and-take of the slippery road, to the itch-and-flush of my cheeks.

The sun is starting to set behind us, which, under different circumstances, would be a magnificent sight. But for now, it just means poorer visibility. Our worn tires, which will fail inspection in a week, offer us little traction, and I am driving with one hand on the emergency brake.

Our one-year-old begins to cry, probably hungry or needing to be changed. My wife, who is wedged between our daughters, starts singing, *Row, row, row your boat*, in her calmest and most soothing voice, but it feels like the wrong music for the occasion. I don't want to imagine a boat floating gently down the stream while we inch our way desperately up this narrow mountain pass.

Papa, my three-year-old says.

Yes, I say.

Are we here yet? she says.

Almost, I say. *Almost.*

But my mind is as slippery as the road, and I soon find myself thinking back to my childhood when, driving home with some family friends, a drunk driver slammed into our car, and how after we spun into a pole and came to a stop, I just sat in the back seat watching that little plastic Hawaiian figure—that had somehow stayed suctioned to the dashboard—keep dancing and dancing.

There was something so strange about watching her do the hula while my friend's father moaned in pain, and I remember wanting to say something about it, wanting to point out that it felt like the entirely wrong detail for the occasion, wanting to ask if anyone else found it ironic. It was as though, even before I knew what poetry was, my twelve-year-old mind was looking to turn this moment into a poem, fascinated by the way a random detail could upend the dramatic narrative, by the uneven mix of tones, by the surreal swirl of terror and the absurd.

Papa? my daughter says, her voice striking me like a Zen master's stick, bringing me back to the present moment.

Yes, I say, tightening my grip on the wheel.

When are we going to get here?

Soon, I say. *Very soon.*

Though I can't help but wonder if my monkey mind is capable of ever being fully here or if I will always be traveling back and forth between the *here and now* and *there and then.*

Dusk has settled into night, and all I can see is the giant red blur of taillights in front of us. My wipers are stuttering against the giant clumps of snow. My one-year-old begins to whimper.

I need to concentrate, I tell myself. *If ever there were a time to focus fully on the task at hand, it is now.*

I sit up in my seat. I establish an alert but relaxed posture, my back straight and centered, my chakras aligned. I begin breathing through my nose to steady and stabilize my awareness. I chant quietly in my head as my eyes scan what is directly in front of me.

Papa? my daughter says.

We're almost here, I say, refusing to let go of my focus.

But as though my three-year-old has suddenly decided to abandon Buddhism for postmodernism, decided to trade her pursuit of enlightenment for an irrational love of disjunction, she channels the great gods of randomness and blurts out with casual curiosity, *Papa, do you have a penis?*

And although I am desperately trying to stay focused on the road and only offer a brief but affirmative response, I can feel my concentration starting to glitch again and can't help but feel the faraway pull of a poem as the car in front of us suddenly swerves left and then right, almost skidding its way off the mountain.

Poetry Repair Kits

I RECENTLY CAME across an old file of mine titled *Poems to Plunder and/or Fix*.

I'd meant it as a space to keep those failed drafts I wasn't quite ready to say goodbye to—something I still believe in doing—but the word *fix* struck me as strange and brought up memories of seeing my dog get neutered when I was a child.

And while no one wants to write the kind of verse that humps a stranger's leg, I'm not sure that castrating a poem is the solution either.

The problem is that when you revise a poem—allowing yourself to transcend your initial impulses and commit to truly reenvisioning what that poem might be—there's no such thing as a quick fix.

Often, the revision process feels like trying to repair the zippers on your kid's backpack—the fastening devices slowed to a standstill as you push and pull to no avail.

And yet, if we stop trying to force closure, if we step back and take pleasure in the irony—that the secret to fixing those zippers lies in unfixing them—we might discover an opening.

There are no easy answers, but what I like about the word *fix* is that its meanings contradict themselves—speaking as much to the problem as they do to the solution.

Anyone, for example, who has ever tried to save a couple of hundred bucks by attempting to repair that leaking faucet on their own knows how sometimes we go in expecting to fix something small and end up in a much greater fix.

And it is that sense of paradox that keeps us revising, tinkering, and looking for the kinds of problems that language alone—at its strangest and most elusive—can both get us into and out of.

To fix a poem, then, is not to castrate it but to ensure that the language is fertile.

Tell your mother we're in a jam, I recently told my three-year old, *and won't be home for at least a half hour.*

Mama, my daughter said into the phone, *we stuck in jelly.*

It took over an hour for the traffic to clear, but my mind tingled all the way home.

Thirteen Ways of Looking at
Looking

WHEN I write, I often start by looking closely at something—as if trying to see it for the first time. But if I sit with it long enough, there is a moment when *looking at* becomes *looking into*, which is what eventually triggers the beginning of the poem.

★

Looking is different from *seeing*—more of a process rather than a result—and therefore more tentative and uncertain and ultimately more interesting.

★

Every child is an artist, writes Picasso. *The problem is how to remain an artist once we grow up.* Writing poems returns us to the restless imagination of our inner child: we grow tired of looking at the clouds and want, instead, to imagine what they look like.

★

There is something about the scenic overlook—with its sweeping and expansive views—that I don't quite trust. I prefer tension and undertows, the recognition that *overlook* means both *heightened view* and *failing to notice* at the same time.

Of all the ways that we might describe how we employ our sight, *looking* is probably the most generic—nowhere as nuanced as gawking or peeking, staring or scanning.

But unlike all those specific verbs, *looking* has more phrasal versatility. I love the way that it combines with particles and prepositions to form whole units whose meanings can't be understood from their parts.

⋆

We often use *look* to mean *seem*. *This looks pretty straightforward,* we say. But looks can be deceiving, and my favorite writing tends to be filled with discordance—those passages that look like prose but read like poems.

⋆

Good prose, writes Orwell, *is like a windowpane*—the words disappearing as we look through them. But making a window requires an in-depth understanding of the complexities of glass and framing, the importance of hidden springs and weights—how much work it takes to offer a clear view.

⋆

When followed by an infinitive, *looking* refers more to an attitude than action. *I'm looking to write in new ways,* we tell ourselves during a dry spell, knowing that sometimes it's more about getting ourselves into a certain mood than producing anything of worth.

Even when a poem stems from a place of detachment, the very act of writing transforms us from onlooker into witness.

When searching for *le mot juste*, we attend to the many senses of a word—are intrigued by all the implications and contradictions—the way *looks*, for example, refers to both how we perceive and how we appear.

The eye, of course, is not enough, writes Theodore Roethke. *But the outer eye serves the inner eye.* And our best poems offer depth of perception—not just an outlook but a vision.

Whenever I revise a poem, I think about the artistry of actors who can translate pages of exposition, convey the depths of a character, with just a single look.

When I first started writing, I would revise by looking over my drafts—quickly inspecting them for careless errors. But there is something ominous about the word *over*.

And ever since my daughters were born, I've started to think of revision as a way of looking after my drafts—the way a parent looks after a child with tenderness and worry, making sure they're dressed in layers before sending them out into the cold.

The Art of Putting Things Together

L AST NIGHT, my two-year-old spent the evening dropping fistfuls of fried rice from her high seat while singing, *Humpty Dumpty had a great faaaaall!*

I probably should have intervened—taken her bowl away or redirected her. At the very least, I should have stopped making sound effects every time the rice hit the carpet.

But as a poet, I've developed the rather remarkable ability to detach myself from my parental responsibilities and view my kids, instead, as adorable little metaphors.

And there was something about the way that she took all those little grains of rice and squares of tofu, slivers of scallions, and broccoli florets, and transformed them into tiny cannonballs that made me think about the process of metaphor-making and the art of putting disparate things together.

But as I watched my daughter drop the rest of her dinner onto the floor, I realized that it's one thing to put ideas together and another to make them stick.

The carpet looked like a Jackson Pollock painting, splattered with rice and shriveled-up pieces of egg.

And as I glanced around the house—at all the scattered toys and dirty dishes—I started to wonder if *Humpty Dumpty* was actually an allegory: Mother Goose's commentary on motherhood and what it means to be immersed in the never-ending struggle of *putting things back together again.*

Papa, my two-year-old said suddenly. *I got doggies.*

Doggies? I said.

She took my thumb and rubbed it against her nose until something green and slimy stuck to it.

Doggies, she said.

And that's when I remembered this exchange from *Alice in Wonderland*:

> "When I *use* a word," Humpty Dumpty said, in rather a scornful tone, "it means just what I choose it to mean—neither more nor less."
>
> "The question is," said Alice, "whether you *can* make words mean so many different things."
>
> "The question is," said Humpty Dumpty, "which is to be master—that's all."

And I started thinking about poetry and two-year-olds and all the delight and confusion that stems from the relationship between language and meaning.

It reminded me of when my older daughter was two and spent all spring talking about wanting to swim in the kiddie pool.

And when summer finally came, and we put on our suits, and I drove her down to her dream destination, she just stared at all the other toddlers with their swimmy diapers and yellow duckies, then looked up at me with such disappointment and asked: *But where are all the kitties?*

Narrative's Building Blocks

M Y FOUR-YEAR-OLD is in the living room, playing with Magna-Tiles. She is as focused as I've ever seen, paying as much attention to shapes as to colors, aesthetics as to structure.

But I don't have a story until I have two stories, writes Grace Paley, and along comes my two-year-old. It's as though she's just finished watching *Donnie Darko* and is convinced that *destruction, too, is a form of creation.*

My four-year-old steps in front of her sister—protecting her work—and suggests they engage in parallel play.

But my two-year-old is a postmodernist at heart. She fakes left, jukes right, then swipes a square from the bottom of the tower and watches its collapse. *There is no center*, she shrieks. *The center cannot hold.*

My four-year-old should know, by now, that our attachment to the impermanent is at the very root of our suffering, that, as Mihaly Csikszentmihalyi writes, *the important thing is to enjoy the activity for its own sake, and to know that what matters is not the result, but the control one is acquiring over one's attention.*

But she looks at her once magnificent creation, now lying in a pile of ruins, and starts to cry.

I pick my two-year-old up, take her to her room, and tell her that she needs to apologize.

Apologize? she says. *Apologize for what? For reminding this family that "Deconstruction," as Derrida points out, "is not an operation that supervenes afterwards, from the outside," but "is always already at work in the work"? Such is the paradox of progress,* she screams from her crib. *Kill your darlings!*

There's no use trying to reason with a two-year-old, so I pull down the shades and turn off the lights, close the door, and leave.

But she refuses to be punished. She begins rattling her baby Elmo's head against the bars of her crib to what sounds like the tune of "We Shall Overcome."

I go back in and confiscate all her dolls. I want her to understand that vulnerability is at the heart of creativity. I want her to acknowledge how much courage it takes to create something from nothing.

But she is adamant, now, that true courage comes from knowing that our creations are always on the verge of collapse.

I try to convince her that she is suffering from massive cognitive distortions, but she is long past listening to me.

She believes in the transformative powers of art and has transformed her crib into a trampoline. She's jumping wildly now, master of her own private mosh pit, lost in that ecstatic lightness of being.

The Image and Its Meaning

M Y FOUR-YEAR-OLD and I were recently walking to the playground when she noticed a picture of a young girl, not much older than she is, hugging a dog.

Aww, she said, *what a cute puppy.*

I didn't have the heart to explain why a picture like that would be posted to a telephone pole, so I smiled and continued walking when she started to sound out the letters in bold on top of the poster.

And then her face dropped, and she asked, *How did that dog get lost?*

I probably should have offered a quick and hopeful response, but there was something about the dialectics of that moment—her excitement over decoding the words coupled with the awful realization of what those words meant—that turned me inward, got me thinking about poetry and all its strange contradictions and undertows.

My daughter was used to picture books where the image of a dog wagging its tail meant a bowlful of puppy chow. And now here was an image betraying its meaning—a picture of a girl with her arms around her pet, representing desperation and loss.

It reminded me of the way she used to clap her hands with such delight every time she saw the flashing lights of an ambulance and how my favorite poems tend to offer us a similar yoking—*pain of message*, as Donald Hall writes, *and pleasure of body.*

I almost wanted to point this out to my daughter, but when I looked down at her, I saw the deep concern in her eyes, saw that she was on the verge of tears. And so, I decided to lie to her instead, told her that I happened to see that young girl with her dog earlier that morning and that they simply must have forgotten to take down the posters.

My daughter looked at me with a mixture of suspicion and relief, and we continued walking toward the playground, but a few blocks later, we came upon another telephone pole with another poster—of a man standing next to a Jeep that he was trying to sell.

Oh no, my daughter said. *That poor man lost his truck.*

And again, I found myself sinking into a bemused reverie, thinking about imagery and the shifting sands of meaning as my daughter ran ahead toward the empty playground and yelled at me to hurry up so we could spend the rest of the afternoon swinging carelessly side by side.

My Two-Year-Old,
the Great Arsenic Lobster

Intelligence is often the enemy of poetry, because it limits too much, and it elevates the poet to a sharp-edged throne where he forgets that ants could eat him or that a great arsenic lobster could fall suddenly on his head.
—Federico García Lorca

I HAVE SPENT much of the summer playing duck, duck, goose. Unlike the local kiddie pool, which is all chaos and concrete, duck, duck, goose offers us a balance of mayhem and order, conflict and resolution. And in doing so, the game provides us with a glimpse into the foundations of narrative.

Everyone sits calmly in a circle as one child walks around tapping the others on the head, chanting *duck, duck, duck*, until a well-timed *goose!* leads to a great chase. Sometimes the ducker takes the goose's seat; sometimes the ducker ends up in the pickle. Then comes the return to calm and order, everyone sitting crisscross applesauce, as a new round begins.

It's the setup of every sitcom I ever watched as a kid.

The problem, of course, is how quickly this gets boring. Even when a kid offers some variation—calls out, *red, red, blue,* or *peanut butter, peanut butter, jelly*—the thrill is short-lived. Sure, there's some nuance to it all. Too many ducks, and suspense builds like in a Dirty Harry standoff. Too few ducks, and we witness the difference between suspense and surprise. And there's the occasional glimpse into character, too—which kid likes a challenge, and which picks the littlest goose on the block. But for the most part, after a couple of rounds, the game feels about as formulaic as a Hollywood sequel.

Unless you're playing with my two-year-old, who calls the game *duck, goose* and sees it as an opportunity to smack people across the face without repercussions.

She chases the ducker even when she's not picked. When it's her turn to choose a goose, she'll tap someone's head then make a beeline for the street. Later, she'll sit in my lap as I read her favorite book aloud, and—without warning—turn around, yell *goose!*, and slap the glasses off my face. Sometimes, she even plays by herself—taps her own head, then runs around in a circle like a dog chasing its tail.

If duck, duck, goose offers us the foundations of narrative, then duck, goose offers us the pleasures of the irrational imagination.

And while we need foundations and craft and technique when we write, we also need mischief and impulse—so that we write the kind of stuff we'd never have thought of in the daylight hours, stuff that doesn't care about rules, that slaps us across the face when we're least expecting it, then runs away shrieking in delight.

Spiraling Thoughts

MY FOUR-YEAR-OLD is not exactly a huge sports fan. Toss her a football, and she'll stuff it down her shirt and pretend that she's having a baby. If we're watching the game and her cousins break out their touchdown dances, she'll launch into a series of pirouettes and curtsies. Sometimes, when she's supposed to be brushing her teeth, I'll catch her singing in front of the mirror, *I'm a pretty flower, such a pretty flower.*

So, what a surprise it was this morning when, out of the blue, she asked me to buy her a Patriots jersey.

I hopped immediately into the car and headed on over to the Arsenal Mall, where even the store names—Target, Old Navy, Sports Authority—made me feel like I was on some sort of ancient, heroic, and very manly quest.

But in every quest, Joseph Campbell reminds us, a hero must undergo a series of tests and trials, and after circling a parking lot of great labyrinthine complexity, I soon found myself facing plundered sales racks and monstrous price tags, duped by a teenaged sorcerer who promised to check the stock out back, then donned a cloak of invisibility.

And as I stood in front of the ancient ruins of a Foot Locker, whose gates were now forever locked, I began to worry that my journey had been a failure.

Fortunately, *the real reason for a quest* never *involves the stated reason*, Thomas Foster tells us. *The real reason for a quest is always self-knowledge.*

And it was just as I was getting ready to drive home empty-handed that I suddenly heard a high-pitched noise coming from the clearance rack at Marshalls. I looked behind me, and there it was—a bright blue Elsa dress—singing the song of the sirens, its small red tag declaring a deep, deep discount, and I realized that maybe this mission wasn't about helping my four-year-old transform into a football fan. Maybe it was really about me learning to accept my daughters for who they are.

And so, it was—much to the dismay of my wife—that I returned home just before kickoff, not with a football jersey, but with so many sequins that the entire living room sparkled *until everything*, as Elizabeth Bishop writes, *was rainbow, rainbow, rainbow!*

The problem with self-actualization, though, is that it's nearly impossible to be a prophet in your hometown. For after my four-year-old hugged me and thanked me profusely for her new dress, she ran right over to the toy bin, grabbed the Nerf football, and asked if I wanted to play—as though she was still trying to please the old me, the *me* of a few hours ago.

And I began to worry that satori meant nothing anymore—that we were knee-deep in a world of sanctioned violence and pom-poms, in an age that valued knowledge over awareness.

By the time we're thirty-five, I once heard Stephen Dunn say, *we all need to find our essential faces.* But before I could warn my four-year-old that she only had thirty-one years left, she stuffed the football down her shirt.

OK, she said to her little sister. *You be the flower girl. Me and Papa are getting married.*

And I looked at her—this tiny little muse who somehow always returns me to my stable self—and was so grateful that she was the one with the ball.

All right, I said. *Break on three.*

Learning to Mine
Those Everyday Moments

I'M BETWEEN poems this morning, which always makes me feel a little lost and anxious, like a puppy waiting for his owner to return home, so I start flipping through an old notebook where I used to gather inspirational quotes.

Every morning I jump out of bed and step on a landmine, writes Ray Bradbury. *The landmine is me. After the explosion, I spend the rest of the day putting the pieces together.*

But reading this only adds to my disquiet, makes me wonder if I'm spending more and more time between poems these days because my life has grown too tame.

After all, when I jumped out of bed this morning, I didn't step on a land mine. I stepped on a small plastic princess and had to flail silently about so as not to wake my wife and daughters.

And I begin to worry that the domestic life has domesticated my imagination.

I start flipping through my notebook to see if I can find some inspiring quotes about changing diapers or doing dishes or cutting the crust off peanut butter and jelly sandwiches.

Creativity is piercing the mundane to find the marvelous, writes Bill Moyers.

That could work, I think. I have my thumb on the pulse of the mundane. But after spending twenty minutes working on a poem titled, "Searching for Blue Sippy, the Sippy Bottle That My Daughter Misplaced and Cannot Live Without," I decide to keep on thumbing.

The best time for planning a book, writes Agatha Christie, *is while you're doing the dishes.*

I like this quote but would like it even more if Agatha Christie explained when the best time for *writing* said book was.

We should always do something that makes us feel like a child, writes Rita Dove, and for a moment I consider walking around the house and pulling all the books off the shelves, then leaving them on the floor for someone else to pick up.

But instead, I keep flipping and flipping and flipping until I find this one by Robert Bly: *When a contemporary man looks down into his psyche, he may, if conditions are right, find under the water of his soul, lying in an area no one has visited for a long time, an ancient hairy man.*

That is it, I think.

I have lost touch with my ancient hairy man and need to delve deep into my psyche to reconnect with my inner brute, need to rescue *the Wild Man* from the caverns of my soul, need to unleash my untamed—

Papa, my four-year-old says from behind me. *Can you come downstairs and make us some pancakes with those little M&M's in them?* I look up and see her reflection in the window and realize that my window to write is now over.

I take my daughter's hand and we walk downstairs where my two-year-old is drawing all over the kitchen tiles with purple Sharpies. I heat up a pan, throw in a pat of butter, and begin searching through the cabinets for leftover Halloween candy. And I start to worry that I will never write another poem.

Writing is utter solitude, writes Kafka, *the descent into the cold abyss of oneself.* But I can't even pee these days without my two-year-old banging on the door, begging to watch me make bubbles.

The butter starts to turn from sizzle to burn, and I can't help but see this as yet another metaphor for my life that I don't have time to explore.

But *when one is highly alert to language*, James Tate writes, *then nearly everything begs to be a poem.*

My two-year-old walks over to my four-year-old and rips the *Frozen* microphone out of her hands. *Mine*, she yells. *Mine!*

And as though my kitchen has turned into a minefield, not so unlike Ray Bradbury's, suddenly things start to explode.

How to Teach Poetry like a Boss

WHENEVER I GET READY to teach a poetry course, my very first step involves doubting everything that I know. I hear the word *qualifications* and think not of *accomplishments* but of *reservations*.

Because even though I have been leading poetry classes for close to twenty years now, even though I wake up early to read and write poetry every single morning of my life, I have no idea how to actually teach it.

Poems can be hard to understand if we're not used to reading them. They can be hard to understand even if we are used to reading them. They often require multiple readings and our undivided attention. Instead of compelling characters and dramatic story lines, they offer us interior landscapes and surprising associative leaps, words playing off one another in charged but subtle ways.

Then comes the challenge of finding the right poems for a particular class—poems that will speak to their emotional and philosophical concerns, poems that will both trouble and console them. Not to mention there's the difficulty of fostering an environment where the classroom truly feels like a community, where everyone feels connected, supported, and challenged in order to take the creative risks to share their work (in its many phases) with others.

You can teach craft, of course, or offer the context behind various movements, or discuss the importance, say, of embracing contradictions.

But poetry has always felt incredibly private to me. I wake up well before dawn every morning to read and write poems for reasons that I'm not sure I could fully articulate. I often have no idea what I'm doing or why I'm doing it—and that's what makes it exciting. I sit down with half-formed ideas and tangled feelings and a cup or three of coffee, and, well, I'm not really sure what happens after that. That's not exactly great fodder for teaching.

I think, though, that in my ideal world, teaching poetry would feel something like this:

A few weeks ago, my four-year-old had *a really, really bad tummy ache* and *really, really needed* to not go to preschool, which meant spending the day with me while I taught my creative writing classes. She was thrilled about this until she actually got to my school and saw how big my students were. She clung to me after that, her head buried in my chest, and refused to let me put her down.

By the second class, she'd relaxed enough to watch some YouTube videos on my computer while I taught. And as she grew less and less self-aware, she started turning up the volume on the computer, singing along to her favorite *Hairspray* songs and dancing in her seat.

My students quickly figured out that if my daughter caught them staring at her, she would shrink back behind the screen. So instead, they snuck glances, not so much listening as overhearing, as my daughter's shyness gave way to joy and she crooned from her seat: *Mama, I'm a big girl now.*

I want teaching poetry to feel like that. So that for a brief while the classroom feels like an incredibly human place—filled with love and vulnerability, fear and laughter and song—so that my students and I can just kind of smile at one another, knowing that there's nothing to say and that there is a great weight to that kind of silence.

On SparkNotes

A STUDENT OF mine recently asked me to write an op-ed article on SparkNotes for my school newspaper. I immediately agreed; however, this posed a slight problem, as I had never actually read SparkNotes. How was I supposed to have an informed opinion about something that I knew very little about? That would be like trying to write a paper on a book that I hadn't actually read.

I realized then that I needed to go on a journey, a journey to discover whether SparkNotes was good or bad. I thought I would turn to *The Catcher in the Rye*, my favorite book from my teenage years, as a litmus test. Would the Notes delight me with the depth of their soulful insights, or would they confirm my worst fears by providing reductive analyses?

There was only one way to find out.

I turned on the classroom computer and visited the SparkNotes website, clicked on *The Catcher in the Rye*, and started to read the plot overview. It seemed mostly accurate, I suppose. Nothing I could really argue with. But it read like the procedure section of a lab report. First, this happened, then that. Where were all the masked insecurities of Holden's voice? Where was his desperation to understand a changing world?

I decided I better move on to the next section, Analysis of Major Characters, but before I clicked on the forward arrow, I found myself drawn to the advertisements flashing all over the page. Beats by Dre, Weight Loss by Jillian, and IRAs by Vanguard—which made me pause to wonder what fifteen-year-old skimming SparkNotes ten minutes before class was considering long-term retirement plans.

I soon remembered my mission and proceeded to Analysis of Major Characters. I was hopeful as I started to read about Holden Caulfield, remembering the way that he struggled to make sense of the precariousness of relationships, the way he wrestled with the existential turmoil of adolescence.

And then I read this: *A caul is a membrane that covers the head of a fetus during birth. Thus, the caul in his name may symbolize the blindness of childhood or the inability of the child to see the complexity of the adult world.*

I thought of the Billy Collins poem—where students tie poems to chairs and beat them with hoses to find out what they really mean—then turned off the computer and crawled into a fetal position of my own.

The truth is, I understand why students might be tempted to rely on SparkNotes. We live busy lives. It is hard to slow down and navigate abstractions. We feel the pressure to be certain even when a book is directing us toward uncertainties. But I also believe in the pleasures of deep introspection and imagination, and I became an English teacher with the hopes of sharing these pleasures with my students. I want them to read and read and read until they find a book that, as Kafka writes, serves as *an ice axe that breaks the sea frozen inside us.* And then I want them to read some more.

So, in many ways, the Notes failed me. I was promised sparks, then handed wet matches. I learned what happened to Holden Caulfield but never experienced my own hopes and despair wrapped up in his, never felt the desire to rip out my favorite page and put it in my pocket before returning the book to the library.

But in other ways, my journey to SparkNotes led me to new discoveries. I may not have found Kafka's *ice axe*, but I did sign up for a new weight loss plan with Jillian and purchased some sweet Beats by Dre.

Now if I could just find someone to explain what all these lyrics mean.

Trashy Lit.

Back in high school, I would spend my weekends rummaging through the book swap at the local dump, convinced that one man's litter was another man's literature.

The books were housed in an old musty shed under a large sign that said, *Free Books*, which I liked to think of as a command—all those trapped classics staring at me like puppies at the pound.

★

My friends used to make fun of me for reading so much. *What are you up to this weekend?* they'd ask. *Vonnegut*, I'd say. *Maybe Baldwin.* They'd always try to convince me to come out with them instead. *C'mon*, they'd say, *let's go get trashed.*

But even then, that struck me as an unpleasant image, and I preferred to use more environmentally friendly expressions. I would grab a can of Natty Light later that night and tell my buddies, *Let's get recycled tonight.*

★

There's something about recycling that feels essential to poetry: the process of stripping language down—attending to its sounds and senses, rhythms and textures—before transforming it into new material.

Makes me wonder if Reduce, Reuse, Recycle is simply the environmentalist's way of saying: *Kill your darlings, steal like an artist, make it new.*

★

Last night, I was sorting through piles and piles of my daughters'
artwork—trying to figure out what to keep and what to throw away—
when I came upon a mouse sitting in the recycling bin beneath the
kitchen sink. The spoils of last night's dinner were just a few feet away,
and here he was, feasting on old scraps of paper.

Poetry, for me, always originates from that feeling of being in the
wrong bin.

★

But even if poetry originates from feelings, it is made entirely out of words.

★

Once, in the alleyways of Kathmandu, I came upon a handful of puppies
that had died in the night and been swept into a pile of trash. It was
disquieting to see them lying there among the banana peels and soggy
rice—their bodies still warm, necks not yet stiff.

Later, trying to write about it, I felt the strangeness of language
haunting me—that the word *litter* could refer to both the newborn
puppies and the strewn trash at the same time.

★

When I first started teaching, I used to run in the early mornings, and
the streets were always empty aside from this one older woman who was
always rummaging through recycling bins for cans and bottles.

And again, I was struck by the strangeness and beauty of language—
that the process of digging through old material and finding stuff worth
saving could be called *redemption*.

Writing Practice

I'VE BEEN THINKING lately about how much of my relationship to writing is contained within the many definitions of the word *practice*.

Some days, writing feels like the kind of practice that a doctor or lawyer might speak of—not just a hobby but a profession. I wake up a few hours before my wife and kids and write with clear goals in mind. I'm aware of deadlines and book sales. I network.

There are benefits to this, of course, but it also beckons my ego in ways that I don't particularly like. I feel a discomforting need for validation. If I'm not careful, I just might start Googling myself.

Other days, it's as though I've channeled my inner Allen Iverson. *Practice? We're talking about practice.* The whole morning is a giant scrimmage, without pressure or urgency, crowds or clocks. I read random articles on ESPN and convince myself that it's all material.

Writing, then, feels like an exploratory process of discovery. But I'm also a step away from becoming that kid who slacks off when the coach isn't looking, who needs the competition of another team to play at his best.

And then there are those days when writing feels like a centering practice—the kind of ritual that keeps me grounded and engaged in the world. I enter a relaxed but focused state of mind, where images and ideas play with one another. I find portals within the language. Everything feels interrelated.

And for a few hours before the sun rises and the bustle begins, I understand what Frost means when he describes *the work* as *play for mortal stakes*.

Playing with Matches

WE'RE LATE for school, and my five-year-old is getting undressed.

We gotta go, I say.

Sorry, she says. *My underwear doesn't match my sweater.*

Does it really matter? I say.

She looks up from the hamper, raises a single eyebrow, then continues digging through the dirty laundry.

And although I'm tempted to point out that no one will ever know whether the trimming of her underwear matches the flowers on her sweater, that chances are she's going to take off her sweater the second she gets to school, as a poet, I understand the importance of such hidden patterns.

A poem is an instant of lucidity in which the entire organism participates, writes Charles Simic, and there's something about metaphor in conversation with form, imagery playing off diction, that feels essential to the workings of a poem.

And yet, I'm wary of anything that fits too neatly together, that feels too tightly orchestrated.

Earlier this week, my five-year-old pirouetted herself into a wall, and hearing her cry, my two-year-old came running over to the rescue.

Put these on your boo-boo, she said, handing her a box of tampons.

There is something about disjunction that is at the heart of both poetry and parenting; it speaks to the way our lives are filled with interruptions and non sequiturs, how my wife and I discuss the stresses of our jobs between bouts of shaking the sillies out.

Last night, as I was putting my daughters to sleep, my five-year-old said, *I love you so much it makes my heart burst.*

Then my two-year-old announced from the other side of the room, *I love you so much, and I like to play with toads.*

And I was reminded of why I wake up so early every morning to read and write poems—with all their imprecise meanings and tangling of tones.

The Education of a Poet

OUR FIRST few steps into Great Meadows establish a big old host of false expectations: two red-winged blackbirds greet us with their trills, and a sunning bullfrog croaks a big fat welcome from his lily pad.

My daughters are delighted, of course, but I find the whole thing kind of unsettling. How am I supposed to secretly train them to become poets if the treasures of nature just reveal themselves so willingly?

I had brought them to this marsh so that we could practice the art of slowing down, sit by the banks and observe the *nothing that is not there*, as Wallace Stevens writes, *and the nothing that is.*

But my five-year-old is skipping up and down the dirt path, twirling in her dress, looking at some spotted turtles that just happen to be plodding across the path.

And my three-year-old is on a mission to see how many rocks she can stuff into my pockets when I'm not looking.

I begin to worry that my kids aren't properly learning to suffer the boredom of childhood when my five-year-old sulks on over—we've been there ten minutes already, and she still hasn't seen a single muskrat.

I sense an opening—a chance to teach her the quiet pleasures of sitting still with heightened attention. We sit down with our legs dangling over the bank, but after ninety seconds of watching the reeds not rustle, she looks dejected.

Even when a large black snake slithers by, all she sees is *not-a-muskrat.*

In this world there are only two tragedies, writes Oscar Wilde. *One is not getting what one wants, and the other is getting it.*

And I start to worry, now, that seeing a muskrat will only disappoint further—that even if we do spot this semiaquatic rat with a peculiar smell, it will never compare to the elusive, magical rodent in her mind.

All these complex and nuanced emotions are often at the heart of great poems, of course, but I also know that, in order to persevere through the uncertainties of the creative process, as Teresa Amabile points out, sometimes you have to stop and celebrate *the power of small wins.*

So I pause and remind my five-year-old of all our accomplishments so far. I start listing all the wonderful wildlife that we have already seen. *Frogs*, I say. *Blackbirds, turtles, snakes, mosquitoes—*

Walruses, my three-year-old blurts out from behind us.

Walruses? I say, turning around.

Yes, my three-year-old says, nodding her head with great assurance. *Very little walruses.*

My five-year-old starts cracking up, and as I watch her return to her joyful and curious self, I realize that maybe I've been going about my mentoring in the wrong way.

I've been trying to teach my daughters to pay solemn attention to the world, when I should be celebrating the wonders of their imaginations, their unwavering belief in the absurd.

After all, if there is such a thing as transcendence, then this is it: all three of us skipping up and down the dirt path, twirling, weighed down only by the rocks in our pockets.

Everything I Know about Literature
I Learned from My Daughters

On Kafka's long-lasting appeal

MY FIVE-YEAR-OLD puts my hands together as if I were praying. She opens them up and asks: *Would you like a fruit punch or a milkshake?*

A fruit punch, I say.

Here's some fruit, she says. Then she taps me lightly on my shoulder.

And here's your punch.

I am about to make a joke about punch lines when my three-year-old runs on over. She puts my hands together and asks: *Do you want chocolate or raspberries?*

Chocolate, I say.

Here's your chocolate, she says. Then she slaps me across the face.

And there's your punch.

*On what Keats might mean when he says,
"man is capable of being in uncertainties . . .
without any irritable reaching after fact and
reason."*

Every evening, the same debate during dinner: my three-year-old arguing with my five-year-old about who is older.

On why we still read the Greek classics

When I get older, my three-year-old says to me, *I want to marry you.*

I'm already married to Mama, I say.

Yes, my three-year-old says. *But when Mama dies, you'll need a new wife.*

On the wise men of Chelm

My five-year-old likes to change her outfit every hour, which would be fine if she hung her dresses back up, if she didn't just toss them on her bed or throw them in the laundry.

Finally, I make a rule that she cannot change outfits for the rest of the day.

An hour later she is wearing something new.

I see that you changed outfits, I say.

I wanted to wear shorts, she says, *so I could be like you.*

I'm not wearing shorts, I say.

You could change, she says.

In Brief

*H*ELP, MY THREE-YEAR-OLD yells, tugging on my leg. *There's a monster under there!*

Under where? I say.

And then she falls to the ground laughing, having made yet another unsuspecting adult say *underwear* aloud. Underwear is a big deal to my three-year-old—a source of both great silliness and pride—which strikes me as fascinating, given how often I have panicked dreams of standing in front of a small audience only to realize that I'd forgotten to wear pants.

And yet, when I first started writing, I thought of poetry as the literary equivalent of taking off your clothes—I would confuse the words *express* and *expose*. It would be years before I understood what Stephen Dunn means when he writes, *The good poem simultaneously reveals and conceals.* Though now that I've reached a certain age, I'm more interested in revelatory details than revealing ones.

A friend of mine recently sent me a card that read: *Congrats, you've reached the halfway point between diapers and Depends.* But *depends* has always struck me as such a strange word—offering connotations of both *trustworthiness* and *uncertainty* at the same time.

Can we ever depend on a poem to just mean what it says?

It depends.

For even when a poem's meaning is clear as day, along comes language like a three-year-old in the middle of the night, poking us awake. *Look*, the poem calls to us. *The meaning is right here. No, wait, now it's under there.*

And so, we keep searching and searching, leaving no phrase unturned, unsure by now if some great epiphany is awaiting us or if the poem is just trying to get us to say, *Under where?*

What I've Learned about Writing from Cartoons

M Y FIVE-YEAR-OLD is obsessed with *Kung Fu Panda*. However, the scratches all over my neck are not from her best impersonation of Master Tigress but are due to the fact that every time we watch the movie, she gets so scared that she clutches onto me for dear life.

I thought that it might alleviate her fears if we watched some behind-the-scenes videos of how the movie was made, and she loved seeing Jack Black dance around the microphone, as animated as his animated counterpart.

The second clip that we clicked on, though, was of three editors examining a scene frame by frame to make sure that the sound effects perfectly matched the images of Po jiggling down a mountain. I was amazed by how complex and precise a process it was, though it only took about thirty seconds before my five-year-old asked if we could go back to watching *that funny guy with wild eyes*.

Seeing these clips, though, reminded me of the saying that a movie is made three times—once by the screenwriter, once by the director, and once by the editor—and got me thinking about how this plays out in the world of poetry and prose.

When we write with Screenwriter Mind, we know that much of what we produce won't end up in the final cut. This can be frustrating, of course, but it can also feel liberating to write without the pressure of getting every scene perfect.

For once we hand that initial draft over to Director Mind, we know that he's probably going to craft every scene from seven or eight different angles, encourage extemporization, and embrace what George Saunders describes as *the improvisatory energy [of] figuring out how [we] get from one marker to the next.*

It's dynamic and thrilling because, at this point, it's still not about getting it right; it's about collecting footage and playing with possibilities.

Then comes Editor Mind. Editor Mind is a control freak except without a sense of humor. Editor Mind has an autographed picture of Gordon Lish on his wall and a pencil drawer filled with erasers. Editor Mind used to be a tax attorney but wanted a career with a little less excitement.

The challenge, then, in writing—where you often have to play all of these roles by yourself—is figuring out how to transition between these very different mindsets throughout the creative process.

One thing I've learned over the years is to try to keep Editor Mind at bay for as long as I can. It can be tempting, at times, to send him dailies, but nothing freezes Screenwriting Mind as much as having Editor Mind looking over his shoulder.

On the other end, it's also important to try to keep Director Mind out of the editing room until he's no longer attached to his work, no longer cares about how much he paid for a cameo or how hard it was to get certain shots.

Better to lock all that footage away, once you're done shooting, and let Director Mind move on to the next thing. Director Mind is relentlessly interested in this world—give him a week off and a cup of strong coffee, and he's ready to immerse himself in an entirely new project.

And once Director Mind has spent a few months on something new, you can break out the old footage from the previous project so that Editor Mind can make the hard decisions of what to cut, reorder, and fine-tune without Director Mind constantly interfering.

It's not easy keeping all these mindsets separate or constantly transitioning between them, but it's also what keeps writing interesting—this complex and dynamic process that demands we each bring our full self, or perhaps many selves, to whatever we create.

Beginnings, Middles, and Middles

I'VE BEEN THINKING lately about how important daily routines are when you have little kids and how those routines both reflect and shape our understanding of dramatic structure.

We rise early in the morning, slowly move into a range of activities until some small inciting incident spurs the day forward, and from there on out, things progress until the climax of dessert, then settle into a dénouement via bedtime routines.

But last weekend, my family headed up to Maine for days filled with canoeing and cousins, swimming and somersaults, and our routine was so disrupted that on our first day there, my daughters somehow got away with eating cheese sticks and ice cream for dinner.

And before we knew it, it was ten o'clock at night, and the window for putting my three-year-old to sleep had jammed shut.

We had deviated from Freytag's pyramid, and now every climax simply begat a need for higher climaxes.

We tried rubbing my three-year-old's back and singing some quiet lullabies, desperately trying to move her along into the third and final act of the day. But she was too busy pinching her sister, licking my elbow, and cuddling with her squeaky dolphin.

My wife and five-year-old closed their eyes and tried to ignore her, but that only made things worse.

Hoping to trigger a resolution, I shifted into idle threat mode—told her I was going to get up right now and drive her back to Boston, throw all her jelly beans away, turn Dolphy into fishing bait in the morning.

But that just made her pinch harder, cuddle louder, and lick wetter.

And I began to worry that this story would never come to a gradual end, that we had shifted into some surreal world where Barth and Beckett ruled, where the dramatic structure of narrative was no longer relevant.

A story can take you through a whole process of searching, seeking, confronting, through conflicts, and then to a resolution, writes Maxine Hong Kingston. But I was convinced that this story would never get past its conflicts.

My only hope was to give up hope, and it was just as I had resigned myself to an entire night of listening to "Where Is Thumbkin?" that I noticed the loons yodeling their moans across the lake.

Shhh, I said, pressing my ear to the window screen.

What is it? my three-year-old asked.

Monsters, I said.

I knew that was wrong as soon as it came out of my mouth. But it was almost eleven o'clock.

And if we're not quiet, I continued, *those monsters are going to come get us.*

I was sure my wife would disapprove. She works with young kids and knows the long-lasting psychological effects of childhood fears.

But she had somehow fallen sound asleep.

And I'm sure there are postmodernists out there who would tell me that stories don't need to follow some stupid pyramid anymore—that some tales are over before they begin, and some are meant to go on forever.

But I'm a traditionalist, at heart. I believe in dramatic arcs and Aristotelian structures—that *a whole is that which has a beginning, middle, and end.*

And I believe, too, in the power of the imagination—how it can turn the song of a loon into something much, much darker, how I could close my eyes and pretend that my three-year-old was clutching so desperately onto my arm, now, because she really wanted to cuddle.

On Winning and Losing

M Y DAUGHTERS have been playing quietly for a good ten minutes, which is always a cause for alarm.

After following a trail of graham cracker crumbs, I finally find them in the bathroom, where my three-year-old is sitting on the toilet and my five-year-old is sitting on the floor in front of her—the two of them holding hands, rocking back and forth, singing *Row, row, row your boat.*

It is a delightfully strange sight made even stranger when my three-year-old looks up at me and declares: *I win!*

I'm used to losing games I didn't even know I was playing, but I can't help but think: *Win what?*

And yet, how often, when writing, I find myself lost in the delightfully strange world of my imagination, rocking back and forth between song and thought, only to look up with a sudden worry about winning. And before I know it, I'm on Amazon checking book sales, on Goodreads looking up ratings.

The problem with winning, though, is that it only begets the desire to win bigger, win faster. If anything, it gets in the way of writing. Not that anyone enjoys losing, but at least our brushes with defeat remind us of what's at stake.

The other night, my daughters were cuddling themselves to sleep, which would have been so much more adorable if my three-year-old weren't such an aggressive cuddler, if she didn't keep slapping her older sister awake.

I quickly shifted into counting-to-three mode, and my three-year-old made it to two in record time.

There's something about the zone between two and three that exerts a certain pressure on the imagination. On bad days, it turns us cautious: we check our swings only to be called out on strikes anyway.

At other times, that border can feel more like a frontier. After all, *trouble*, as Terrance Hayes reminds us, *is one of the ways we discover the complexities / of the soul.*

I imagine that this is what my three-year-old must have been thinking when she raised first her palm and then a single eyebrow, then yelled *Three!* and got one more slap in before running off to her own bed.

Unleashing Your Creative Flow

FOR MANY YEARS now I have woken up early every morning to write for a few hours before the day officially begins.

But a few weeks ago, my family and I decided to take a road trip from Boston to South Carolina. And because my daughters can't seem to make it more than twenty minutes in the car without asking when we are going to get there, I thought it might be best to skip my morning routine in order to drive while they slept.

I was hesitant, at first, about giving up writing for even just a few days—and channeling Henry James, worried that I would turn irritable, become *one of those people on whom* everything *is lost*.

But there is something about driving that seems to speak to the creative process, and as we left Massachusetts, I found myself entering a familiar state—my mind wandering from one idea to the next—and soon the empty highway began to feel like the open road.

For me, writing is often about getting myself into a certain mood, one filled with mischief and introspection, until my mind begins to tingle and some scrap of language or half-formed idea startles me toward the start of a poem.

But as I finished the last sip of coffee from my oversized travel mug, I realized that said tingling had descended from my mind down to my bladder.

There were plenty of rest stops along the highway, but to pull over was to risk waking my wife and daughters, and I wasn't sure that I was ready to give up my morning reverie.

It was then that I noticed an empty plastic bottle beneath my wife's seat.

I could feel my mind squirming with possibility.

But as I began plotting out how exactly I was going to pull this off, I felt the same hindering doubts that emerge every time I start a new poem: *what if things take off in a very different direction?* Or, perhaps even worse, *what if I get terribly, terribly stuck?*

I started imagining all the possible ways that things could go awry and immediately started scanning highway signs for the next rest stop. And yet, as much as I was tempted to play it safe, it's the insistent uncertainty—the exploration of the unknown—that makes writing so thrilling in the first place.

And so, it was with the clouds just starting to turn pink and my wife and daughters breathing heavily beside me that I managed to do the only thing I know how to do as a writer—get myself into a hole and hope that hole turns out to be some sort of portal.

Poetry makes nothing happen, Auden famously wrote, and peeing into that Gatorade bottle probably saved me, at most, about six minutes on I-90. But it also granted me another couple of hours before anyone asked if we were there yet.

And more importantly, it gave me the chance to feel like I was writing even when I wasn't writing—offering me that strange mix of urgency and awkwardness, vulnerability and alertness, and the opportunity to attend to pressing internal matters while experiencing the ecstasy of flow.

Passports to Wonders and Miracles

I T HAD BEEN two weeks of unbearably hot and muggy weather. My five-year-old suggested that we cool off by heading to the library, which made me worry that she was beginning to think of our local branch not as *an arena of possibility*, as Rita Dove writes, or as a space filled with *passports to wonders and miracles*, as Libba Bray writes, but as that place with central air.

Still, I, too, was desperate for AC. And luckily, not only was the library air-conditioned, but it also happened to be hosting a live animal program for kids. And maybe I was just trying to justify our outing in my mind, but I couldn't help but notice how literary the entire event felt.

In fact, if it weren't for all the people in the room, it would have reminded me very much of a poetry reading—with a bearded sage standing in front of us looking like Percy Bysshe Shelley's *unacknowledged legislator of the* animal *world*.

The first creature on display was an umbrella cockatoo, a rather feathery bird that danced like Chris Kattan in *A Night at the Roxbury*. And although we all laughed in delight, it reminded me of the poems I used to write when I first started writing—funny and offbeat, but also completely tame and inclined to imitate.

Next came the kinkajou, and my daughters clapped when it hung upside down to eat half a banana out of the teacher's hand. There was something to admire in its sense of theatricality and willingness to perform, but I saw in it also my worst tendencies as a writer—that desire to be rewarded for every little clever trick.

We were ready now for something a little more dangerous, and before we knew it, we were staring at a real, live tarantula. We all *oohed* and *aahed* and scooted back a little bit as the spider sat there doing absolutely nothing.

It got me thinking about how often I rely too heavily on the ideas behind a poem instead of attending to the weight and texture of the words in front of me.

The highlight of the show, for my daughters, was the cane toad—at six pounds, it was huge, otherworldly, and most importantly, it peed all over the instructor. Brought to Australia to solve a pest problem, it soon took over the continent: with poisonous bulges around its neck, it was as dangerous to predators as to prey. It was the kind of poem I always wished I could write—absurd and deadly at the same time.

But if the creative life is ultimately a quest for self-actualization, it was the flying squirrel that spoke to my inner self.

There is another world, writes Paul Éluard, *but it is in this one*. And although the flying squirrel is native to Massachusetts, I'd never actually seen one. Even in that bright afternoon sun, it was hard to catch more than a quick glimpse of it—because every time the teacher brought it out, it skittered across his shoulders to hide in his shirt pocket.

But there was something so intimate about that gesture; it reminded me of why I fell in love with poetry in the first place—how we come to it expecting magnificent flight, and it just wants to hide in that closed-off space closest to our hearts.

Sometimes, When We Pick Our Poems Up

By the time I'd get my poems back . . . I could see them in
a new way, maybe like children getting off the bus from
their first day of school.
    —*Kay Ryan*

SOMETIMES, WHEN WE PICK our poems up, they come sprinting into our arms, and we can't tell if they are overjoyed to see us or if we are rescuing them from the cruelties of the playground.

Sometimes, when we pick our poems up, we don't let them know that we are there, and we watch them through the window with workshop silence.

Sometimes, when we pick our poems up, they're in a different font, and we barely recognize them.

Sometimes, when we pick our poems up, we find ourselves comparing them to all the other poems—wondering why our poems can't do backbends, noticing how none of the other poems have stains all over their shirts.

Sometimes, when we pick our poems up, we see other writers who look like they're working on new poems—but we have learned to never ever never say anything until we actually see those new poems on paper.

Sometimes, when we pick our poems up, they suddenly look all grown up, and we can't believe that just a few weeks ago, they were some tiny scraps of language scribbled on the back of a Starbucks receipt.

Sometimes, when we pick our poems up, they have a meltdown right in the middle of the hallway, and we wish they were final drafts already and not a work in progress.

Sometimes, when we pick our poems up, we see them lined up against the wall and worry that we have tamed all that beautiful wildness right out of them.

Sometimes, when we pick our poems up, we feel so grateful that others have taken the time to understand them, to care for them despite their flaws.

Sometimes, when we pick our poems up, they ignore us and just keep playing with their friends beneath the slide. They've been fending for themselves all day long and are ready to subscribe to *la mort de l' auteur*.

A Loose Truth

IT WAS one of those unseasonably warm evenings earlier this fall when I bit into a beet and my front tooth came loose. It was a false crown to begin with, but I had had it for so long that I had forgotten it wasn't real.

My dentist replaced it with a temporary cap that turned out to be even more temporary than expected, and no matter how firmly he cemented it in place, it kept coming loose.

For the next month, I found myself practicing the art of slow eating, paying close attention to the texture of food, testing each bite's density and pushback. And maybe it was just my ever-insistent existential angst, but every time my three-year-old checked in on my well-being, it sounded like she was asking about my *loose truth*.

There is something about instability that feels intrinsically related to poetry—as though grappling with the looseness of language could help us reconcile our own impermanence. It's no wonder that we encounter poetry most often at liminal occasions—weddings and funerals—those ceremonies that help us mark the passage from one state of being to another.

When my older daughter discovered that her first tooth was loose, she went on a hunger strike, refusing to participate in this unwanted ritual. For a solid week, she wouldn't eat solid food.

And then one night it fell out on its own, and she woke up the next morning with a gap in her mouth and a tiny tooth lodged beneath her tongue.

For the next six hours, she kept that tooth hidden in the back of her mouth without saying a word about it. When she smiled, she smiled with pursed lips. When it was time for lunch, she asked to eat in the privacy of her own room.

And although I worried for her, I tried to think of this as a poetic initiation of sorts.

Forced to accept what we don't yet understand, we wake up knowing that something inside us has changed, and we long for a private space of reckoning. The bad muse tells us to buck up and move on—put the dumb tooth under the pillow and collect our lousy quarter.

But if poetry teaches us anything, it's that we must try to believe in the tenderness of absence, trust that emptiness can also be an opening.

The Art of Overhearing

Take a Sharpie away from my three-year-old, and she will invoke Whitman and begin sounding her *barbaric yawp over the roofs of the world.*

But plop her on the toilet, and the scene is much more reminiscent of the Romantics—as she ponders philosophical questions, her imagination wandering wildly and her intonations somewhere between speech and song.

Just yesterday, she sat on her throne for a good twenty minutes, talking about where we go after we die and making up songs about tortillas. I could have sworn, at one point, she mentioned something about *a host of golden daffodils.*

And as my wife and I stood in the hallway, listening in, I was reminded of John Stuart Mill, who offered us the image of the poet as a solitary figure lost in deep contemplation. *If we may be excused the antithesis,* writes Mill, *we should say that eloquence is* heard; *poetry is* over*heard.*

Yet, there are times when overhearing can feel like an intrusive art: we read a poem, and it feels as though we're spying on a neighbor through their kitchen window, watching them sing into a wooden spoon while they dance in their not-so-tighty-whities.

And there are other times, too, when there's simply too much distance between what the poem whispers and what we can hear—as though the poet lives downstairs from us and has thrown a dinner party without inviting us. We are privy to the sounds of laughter but not to any of the jokes.

My favorite writers seem to know the difference between naked and nude, between understatement and obfuscation. They consider and reconsider life at just the right volume so that others will want to lean in.

In order to strike that balance, though, we first have to learn the art of overhearing ourselves when we write—to quiet all the chatter in our minds so that we can *catch the big fish*, as David Lynch writes, that swims deep within the psyche.

It can be hard to find that kind of quiet.

But on those mornings when we can tune out all the distractions and doubts, we can almost hear what sounds like our essential voice—pondering philosophical questions, our imagination wandering wildly and our intonations somewhere between speech and song.

How Cleaning the Fridge
Is like Revising a Poem

IT ALWAYS BEGINS with that little old cup of leftover beans that's not quite moldy but on its way, or the container of mac 'n' cheese that wouldn't fail the sniff test, per se, but you could use the Tupperware for something else.

Though now that you're looking around, you notice a half-eaten container of prunes. Prunes don't go bad, of course, but they don't go good either. And besides, *to prune* literally means *to remove*, so you might as well get rid of those too.

It feels good to get rid of a little bit of clutter—to cut what can easily be cut—though you should probably call it quits for now before you get yourself into a project.

Still, your kids are quietly playing in the next room, and it's not like you have something better to do. So, you decide to check out the cheese drawer where you find three open packages of the exact same type of shredded cheese.

You consolidate.

And since you've committed to calling it *the cheese drawer* and believe in the importance of *getting the words right*, as Hemingway says, you might as well take out all the items that aren't technically cheese—blackberries, ketchup packets, and a half-eaten scone that disintegrates upon contact.

This, of course, is what you were worried about in the first place because now you have to pull the entire drawer out so that you can shake the crumbs into the sink, and that's when you notice some sort of purple, goopy mess that's pooled in the back-left corner of the fridge.

You clear out the bottom row and find the remains of what looks like a Popsicle that your three-year-old must have stashed back there weeks ago.

You have no choice now but to empty the entire fridge and scrub the thing clean.

You fill up a bucket with warm soapy water and are surprised, not by how disgusting the fridge is, but by how you somehow didn't notice how disgusting it was. You spend half an hour scrubbing and scouring, wiping and drying, and when you are done, it looks so spanking new that you can't help but be more selective about what you put back in.

No need to keep three different brands of yellow mustard or the salad dressing that will expire next month or even the overpriced dark chocolate-covered orange peels that you bought your wife the day before she gave up sugar.

You would have felt wasteful throwing these things away before, but you can almost see Marie Kondo nodding her quiet approval as each *darling* clanks in the trash.

You are working without any sense of attachment now as though this is someone else's fridge. It's no longer about making some small adjustments; it's about reenvisioning your refrigerator as a carefully arranged system of essential items.

But *arranged* isn't quite the right word. This is about orchestration— complementing condiments and juxtaposed jars—about function and design, purpose and aesthetics.

And even though you know that this won't last—that the fridge will soon be inundated with groceries and leftovers—you are grateful for this stolen hour in the middle of the day to bring order to chaos, for this *momentary stay*, as Frost says, *against confusion.*

Poetry and Masks

*T*EAR OFF *the mask,* writes Rumi. *Your face is glorious.* And for a long time, I thought of writing poems as a way of revealing one's most authentic face.

But after reading Robbie Cooper's *Alter Ego*—a book that pairs photographs of people beside their avatars—I started wondering whether writing was more a process of taking masks off or putting them on.

Many of the pairings in Cooper's book offer striking examples of contrast—in gender, age, species, body type—and fascinating personal commentary about what it means to feel like your true self is stuck inside the wrong body.

But many pairings also reveal a clear resemblance between the person and their avatar, with the pixelated figures offering just a little more chisel and curve.

And as I looked at those photos, I couldn't help but wonder if my writing voice was simply a literary version of an avatar—the me that's me but not really me—whose mind is slightly more chiseled, whose logic is just a wee bit curvier.

How often I sit at my desk in the dark, lost in a reverie, contemplating this world with great understanding and empathy. And then the sun rises, and we're suddenly late for work, and my five-year-old spills milk all over her brand-new shirt, and a very different face emerges.

I sometimes wonder if one day, when my daughters are older, they will read my poems and realize that they are finally seeing my truest face.

Or will they think: *Where was this witty, thoughtful man when we used Sharpies to measure all our stuffed animals against the kitchen wall?*

I know that there is no such thing as the true me.

I am large, Whitman reminds us. *I contain multitudes*. But sometimes, particularly in the early stages of drafting, I worry that if my poems were ever to meet me, it would play out like that pivotal scene in *Star Wars: The Empire Strikes Back* where Darth Vader announces to Luke, *I am your father*.

Those drafts would stare at me incredulously, shaking and holding on to an amputated line. *No, no,* they would say. *That's impossible*. And then they would dive into some deep and dark abyss just to escape from me.

And all I can do is hope that one day they will return and approach me with great tenderness as they lift my mask and glimpse my wounded face—knowing that our poems must witness our rawest vulnerabilities if they're going to run off and save this world from itself.

Passage Analysis

T HE SAFETY GATE in our front hallway had been obsolete for a while: my three-year-old had figured out how to unlock it by herself, and for the past few months, we had primarily been using it as a drying rack for wet mittens.

When I finally got around to disassembling it last week, my daughters treated it like the fall of the Berlin Wall and celebrated with some prolonged butt wiggling. My wife, realizing that our baby was no longer our baby, quickly found herself on the verge of tears. And every time I passed the top of the stairwell, I saw an opening in place of a locked gate and couldn't help but sense the start of a poem.

A poem, of course, is made up of *stanzas*, a word that means *rooms* in Italian, but it's the movement between and within those rooms that turns the poem into poetry.

Not a thought, as Morris W. Croll writes, *but a mind thinking.*

I am often struck by how much both my daughters love hallways. Try to settle them inside any single space, and they'll want to escape—longing for that freedom to move about, for the opportunity to bounce between rooms.

My wife is convinced that we need to feed them less sugar, but I like to think of it as part of their initiation to the restless energy of poetry.

Poetry at its most basic level, writes Matthew Zapruder, *is about . . . the leap from one thought to another: what I call the associative movement particular to poetry. That leap, that movement, is what makes poetry* poetry.

This morning, though, after returning home from an extended stay at the playground, my three-year-old made it halfway up the stairs before deciding to plop on down.

Of all places to stop and rest, I thought, *why would someone want to plant their face on a wet and sandy stair?*

But because it's easier to think of my three-year-old as a metaphor than to understand the logic behind her actions, I started thinking about passages—not the ones we write, but the ones we must seek out in order to write—and what it means to dwell in those corridors between inner and outer worlds.

Writing Routines and Mindfulness

WE RECENTLY HAD some friends over for dinner when my three-year-old decided to pass around her latest art project—a flattened toilet paper tube that was supposed to resemble a Fruit Roll-Up. One by one, our friends put down their forks, politely examined her art, praised it, and even pretended to eat it.

Why is it so wet? I asked when it was my turn.

I dipped it in the toilet, she whispered, *so it would stay flat.*

I probably should have leapt right into action and hauled our industrial-sized tank of hand sanitizer up from the basement. But I just sat there, toilet water dripping from my hands, thinking about what a good story this was going to make.

This, of course, is why when a friend of mine recently invited me to write an article for her website about how developing a writing routine can help parents become more mindful, I was immediately filled with great worry: poets aren't exactly known for offering practical advice.

However, I do believe that one of the main reasons that I get up so early to write every morning is that it helps me be a more reflective and attentive parent. Often, I don't even notice how writing affects my state of mind until I've fallen out of my routine. Then I'm irritable and easily frustrated. My five-year-old lies crying on the floor after dinner, and I think: *Why can't I just do the dishes in peace?*

And then I realize that no, she probably didn't pirouette into the wall on purpose. And yes, it has been a few days since I've taken the time to write down my thoughts in a journal or shape some of that raw material into a poem.

There are only the pursued, the pursuing, the busy and the tired, Nick Carraway says in *The Great Gatsby*. When you have little kids, you tend to go to sleep busy and wake up tired. But writing can help you remember the pursuit.

In his book, *Here I Am,* Jonathan Safran Foer writes, *Children ask, "Are we there yet?" Adults: "How did we get here so quickly?"* Most days, I can barely remember why I got up from my desk and wandered into the kitchen, let alone recall all the poignant and bewildering things that my daughters say and do throughout the day. It's only when I take the time to sit down and write that I find myself slowing down and attending to my thoughts and feelings, recording and responding to the events of the day.

But writing isn't just a way of capturing small moments; it's also a way of freeing them. It offers us the private freedom to acknowledge thoughts and emotions that we might not like to admit to having. It becomes a sacred space where we can return to ourselves without judgment or consequence and make sense of complicated feelings. After all, *we do not write to be understood,* writes C. S. Lewis. *We write in order to understand.*

But beyond being a space to process our emotions, writing also offers us tools and devices to transform our experiences into art. We begin by recording some minor frustration about the never-ending piles of laundry, and before we know it, we're meditating on the challenges of sorting chaos into order.

My five-year-old's refusal to eat a sandwich with even a speck of crust still on it is not just another hassle preventing me from getting to work on time; it's an opportunity to meditate on how having children strips away our hardened outer layers and returns us to the softness at our core.

On the days where I'm able to think of writing as a metaphysical practice, as a play space for my daily frustrations and disappointments, I stop resenting all the challenging moments and see them, instead, as potential for creative material.

And yet, given how hectic parenting is, how impossible it is to balance a career and family, let alone find thirty seconds to pee without someone tugging on my leg, how do I suddenly find time to start a writing routine?

Again, I'm not sure that I'm the right person to offer advice, but recently, my three-year-old told me that she's memorized how to drive to her school. *First you go outside*, she said. *Then you get in the car. And then you are there.* And in some ways, I think that starting a writing routine is no more complicated than that. *First, you get some paper. Then you start writing. And then you are a writer.*

Opposable Stubs

FOR HALLOWEEN this year, my younger daughter wants to dress up as Elphaba Thropp, the misunderstood witch from *Wicked*. She thinks my wife should go out as a peach tree with real peaches and tells me that I should dress up as a finger.

There is something about the image of a lone finger wandering the neighborhood that feels both terrifying and delightful—makes me think of Edward Hirsch's description of postmodernism as *a genre of disruption* with its love of *the fragment*.

The true genre of disruption, though, is not postmodernism but parenthood. I don't remember the last time I showered without someone trying to knock down the bathroom door. My younger daughter can barely even finish a sentence these days without interrupting herself.

And yet, as scattered as parenting makes me feel on a daily basis, on the one occasion that I had to spend a single night away from my wife and daughters, I felt so terribly incomplete.

★

I wonder if a lone wandering finger could ever evoke anything other than a sense of loss.

★

And yet, loss is the ultimate catalyst for transformation—one can imagine a detached middle finger, say, reveling in its newfound ability to stand up without others seeing it as an act of aggression.

★

For a long time, I struggled to understand the difference between *detached* and *unattached*, couldn't quite grasp the idea that *detachment* is a form of *apathy*, whereas *nonattachment* is *a process of expanding our empathy*. But stories like *Wicked* help us realize that a single story is never the whole story, that there are holes in the narratives of our youth.

★

Last night, we spent dinner debating whether a straw has one hole or two holes—a discussion that would have felt delightfully dialectical if my daughters weren't simply set on opposing each other's ideas.

★

Not that there's anything wrong with opposition—the thumb, that tiny little opposable stub, is said to have led to the rise of humanity.

Portraits of a Young Artist

*The day is coming when a single carrot, freshly observed, will
set off a revolution.*
　　—Paul Cézanne

I AM COOKING DINNER while my six-year-old sits at the art table,
drawing pictures of winking mermaids, when the tormented spirit
of Van Gogh suddenly swoops in and possesses her body.

I can't work with these lousy crayons, she yells.

I sit down next to her and try to explain that it's the process not
the product that matters. I want her to understand that when we slow
down and take the time to observe something carefully, we *move from
passive absorption*, as Maria Konnikova tells us, *to active awareness.*

I get some blank paper and encourage her to simply look at a
single object and practice drawing what she sees. I tell her not to
worry about how it turns out, that the true joy of any art comes from
learning to pay close attention.

I return to the cutting board and I'm about to start chopping
an onion when my daughter tells me that she really, really needs my
help. I walk back on over to the art table to see what I can do when
she starts grilling me with questions.

Has your head always been so small? she asks, drawing a tiny circle
in the middle of the page. *And how come Mama's teeth are so much
whiter than yours?* she says, reaching for a yellow marker. She adds some

black curls to the top of my tiny head then grabs a white crayon and begins adding gray tones when I pull her paper away and tell her that she has clearly mastered the art of close observation and is ready to move on to something a bit more expressionistic.

I show her some basic swirling techniques and tell her not to worry about accuracy. Instead, I want her to understand that the true *aim of art*, as Aristotle said, *is to represent not the outward appearance of things, but their inward significance.*

She tells me she'll have a go at it and gets to work while I go back to cooking, and for the first time in weeks, a good ten minutes pass by and not a single piece of paper is torn to shreds, not a single marker hurled against the wall.

But when I come over to see what she's working on, I see that she has scribbled out the face in her drawing.

I remind her that we need not be ashamed of our mistakes. After all, *there is no poetry*, Joy Harjo reminds us, *where there are no mistakes.*

That's not a mistake, she says. *That's a picture of you.*

I'm about to ask why my inward significance looks like a plate of thrown-up spaghetti when it occurs to me that perhaps I'm still going about this all wrong.

I've been focused on teaching my six-year-old craft and technique, trying to offer her insights into various historical movements and periods so that she can think of her work in conversation with the masters, when maybe what I really need to do is to help her understand how art is driven by our emotional connection to the work.

So I tell her to forget everything I've told her so far and instead to simply draw a picture of her happy place.

She smiles and pulls out a blank piece of paper while I finish making dinner.

And just as the stew finishes simmering, she presents me with a masterpiece: a near-perfect drawing of her and her sister riding on unicorns and leaping over rainbows. In the bottom left-hand corner is a smiling chocolate swirl of soft-serve ice cream with my name on it.

I praise her flights of fancy and tell her that I'm flattered that she included me in her happy place and that she thinks of me as an ice cream cone.

That's not an ice cream cone, she says.

What is it? I say.

A poop emoji, she says.

I kneel down next to her and try to explain that, as artists, we have the moral responsibility to use our imagination in positive ways.

She tells me that she understands and that she's really, really sorry.

I make her put her markers away and get ready for dinner, but she asks if she can eat at the art table.

Fine, I say, *but no drawing while you eat.* She agrees.

The problem, though, with raising a budding artist is that everything becomes an opportunity for self-expression.

And when it's time to clean up, I can't tell if the uneaten carrots in her bowl are a commentary on my cooking or a tribute to Cézanne and a hint of the *revolution* to come.

Workshops and Mountaintops

I T WAS my four-year-old's first day at her new school, and she was clinging to my leg so tightly that I was beginning to lose circulation. *Don't leave me*, she kept saying, *don't leave me*, as though I was abandoning her at an orphanage.

We knocked on the door. An older woman opened it, and without even knowing my daughter's name, scooped her into her arms and told her that she loved her. She put my daughter down and led her to her cubby, stopping to hug her three more times before they reached the classroom.

My daughter hung up her jacket, put her *blankie* in her bag, then ran off to explore the play area without even glancing my way.

Maybe it was because I was about to teach a writing class, but I couldn't help but wonder what it would be like if workshops worked this way. *The genuine thing in us is much too fragile*, writes Kay Ryan, *to tolerate the kind of peer pressure or superior pressure of most writing programs or workshops*. And yet, how often we show up with a poem that's only half-finished—that's clutching onto us with fear—only to hand it over to strangers to scrutinize.

How empowering would it be if we trusted that the other people in the room were there to greet it with open arms and affirmations, nurture it, and offer it unconditional love? I was imagining what this might look like when the teacher raised her hand for the kids to line up.

This was my cue to leave, and I was about to wave goodbye when a boy—about twice the size of everyone else—walked on over to my daughter and shook his fist in front of her face. And then, in a voice way too deep and gravelly for any preschooler, he said, *I'm really mean.*

I have never wanted to dropkick a four-year-old so badly in all my life.

But I didn't.

I watched my daughter eye this boy up and down, then look right past him, letting him know that she wasn't intimidated, that she wasn't about to come running to me for help.

And I realized that this, too, is what we want when we bring a poem to a workshop.

Our poems are precious to us in ways that no one else will ever understand. We desperately want people to love them and slather them with praise.

But we also want to see that they won't fold under a little scrutiny.

And as I watched my four-year-old stand on her little green circle with such poise and confidence, I couldn't help but think of a former teacher, the poet Ken Rosen, who used to remind the class—whenever he would sense one of us getting defensive—that *the poem must learn to travel to the mountaintop alone.*

Windows and Mirrors

M<small>Y WIFE</small> is in the passenger seat using up the last of her data while my kids read quietly to themselves in the back.

I am enjoying the peaceful sound of the rain while I drive, thinking about this past summer, though *thinking* might be the wrong word. It is more like I am watching thoughts wander aimlessly around my brain.

And even though my thoughts aren't moving all that fast, I can feel them getting winded and watch them slow down in order to stretch, and before I know it, those thoughts are being carried away on a stretcher. Except it isn't a stretcher exactly, but more like a chariot, or maybe a raft floating lazily down a river, the kind of river where you might expect to see big old burgundy mushrooms lining the banks.

It is so peaceful and lovely, and then I am suddenly aware that I am dreaming. And driving. And drifting into the left lane where another car is trying to pass me.

I quickly right the steering wheel and look over at my wife, who is still on her phone and doesn't even register the jerk, then back at my kids who are still reading. And I realize that I must have been asleep for only a second or two, though it felt like much longer.

I reach over and take my wife's hand and tell her that I love her, that I'm sorry for everything and anything, and that I really, really love her.

She asks me if I am OK, and I nod my head.

It is so quiet that all we hear is the rain falling, light and steady on the car.

And I realize this is what writing is like. We go from thinking to dreaming, lose all sense of time and place, of self and being, of being housed in our bodies, until we are jolted awake with urgent awareness.

And when we return to ourselves, our bodies have barely moved, and yet we have been moved deeply, reminded of how tentative our lives are, of what's at stake, of our own agency and flaws.

We look around and realize that we are surrounded by windows and mirrors—that these things can kill us, and that they can save us too.

Anatomy of a Line

MY FOUR-YEAR-OLD has been refusing to eat dinner lately. Sometimes she tells me that she's too tired to eat. Sometimes she protests the tiny specks of color that somehow made it into her meal. Once she tried explaining that *some people are eating people and some people are not.*

At first, I thought I'd let her suffer the natural consequences of her actions. But once I realized that the natural consequences of her actions involved her waking me up at 2:00 a.m. to ask for a bowl of Cheerios, I figured I needed a new strategy.

The other evening, I threatened to cancel dessert for the rest of her childhood if she didn't eat something for dinner.

Fine, she said, staring me down. *I want water with nothin'.*

And as I sat there pondering my next move, I realized that my four-year-old might have very well just uttered a near-perfect line of poetry.

The ear is the only true writer, writes Frost, and this line highlights the relationship between music and meaning.

The first half dances with an alliterative trifecta of Ws—*want, water, with*—that deceives you into thinking that the line is going to be filled with pleasantries.

But said alliteration is undermined by the dramatic repetition of trochees—*water, nothin'*—and those stressed-unstressed feet stomp down like an insolent child.

However, the true beauty of this line is in the way that it plays with familiar patterns of language, manipulating a sentence structure that we normally associate with kids' meals: *I want peanut butter with jelly. I want noodles with sauce. I want ice cream with sprinkles.*

The first half of my daughter's request fools us into thinking that she is going to follow this pattern—*I want water with lemon,* we half expect her to say. Or *I want water with a fresh sprig of mint.*

But instead of following *I want water* with a complementing garnish, she doubles down in order to escalate things to a point of absurdity. And this deviation suddenly changes the meaning of the first half of the line. Water is no longer a cold and refreshing drink but a defiant proclamation of asceticism.

Genuine poetry can communicate before it is understood, writes Eliot, and even before I sat down to consider the formal dimensions of my daughter's comeback, I found myself simultaneously troubled and delighted by it—realized that I was up against a budding master of prosody and craft.

If only I could convince her that she need not be a starving artist.

Rejection Notices

For a long time, whenever I would drop my older daughter off at a birthday party, she would cling to my leg and beg me to stay, promising me half her slice of cake if I promised not to leave.

Then one day I brought her to a classmate's party, and before I knew it, she was off running around with her friends without even waving goodbye—and I just stood there with a dull, nameless pang rooting around in my chest.

It's the same feeling that I get whenever I'm in the middle of writing a poem and begin to feel it slipping away from me.

A poem can be said to have two subjects, writes Richard Hugo, *the initiating or triggering subject, which starts the poem or "causes" the poem to be written, and the real or generated subject which the poem comes to say or mean, and which is generated or discovered in the poem during the writing.*

But I always find it so unsettling whenever I'm between those two subjects—when I realize my original vision for a poem isn't yet fully realized, when I know something is off but I'm not sure what.

Sometimes, I wish that our drafts could just tell us what is wrong, that they were as blunt as my four-year-old who recently told me: *You're my best friend in the entire world. But I wish Tom Brady was my dad.*

But more often than not, a draft will present us with some vague sense of unease—a disquiet that's almost too quiet to hear, a suppressed angst that communicates in hushed tones.

Sometimes, a poem will simply refuse to *click shut*, as Yeats says a poem ought to.

We make it to the final stanza and can't quite compress all that we want to say into a single line or decide between two closing images.

And before long, it becomes clear that it's not just a matter of struggling to put *the best words in the best order*—which is poetry, as Coleridge writes—but that we actually have two poems that want to travel in two separate directions.

At other times, after finishing a draft, we'll come upon a title that would have been absolutely perfect had we written a different poem. And though it would be so much easier to just keep tinkering with those two words on top, some small voice inside us begins whispering something about keeping the title and starting anew.

Sometimes, I wish my poems would just do what I wanted them to do. But their refusal to do so has made me a better listener, forced me to pay closer attention to their textures and tones.

It reminds me of when my daughters were babies and would begin to fuss, and my wife could almost tell immediately, by the pitch of their cries, whether they wanted to be held or whether they needed to be changed.

Labor of Love

WHEN I FIRST STARTED telling friends that my wife and I were pregnant with our older daughter, my wife would shoot me a look to remind me that only one of us, technically, was pregnant.

So, I can't help but feel the pettiest of joys in the fact that my four-year-old happens to believe that, while her older sister was born in the most conventional of ways (uterus, birth canal), she somehow managed to emerge out of my stomach.

Furthermore, every time I tell some story about something that happened back in college, my younger daughter will nod her head and say, *Yeah, I remember that because I was in your belly back then.*

According to my four-year-old, not only did she gestate inside my womb for the typical three trimesters, but she has always, *always* been inside of me.

I can't help but see this as a metaphor for writing.

Most poets write the same poem over and over, writes Richard Hugo, and no matter how much I try to vary my subjects, I always end up tackling the same concerns, delving into the same lifelong mysteries that have always been burning inside me—as though every poem is leading me closer to finding my essential face.

To complicate the matter though, ever since my four-year-old watched *Happy Feet* last year, she has been convinced that, at some point during the pregnancy, I removed her from my womb and placed her inside a penguin egg until it was time to hatch.

And, ridiculous as that sounds, this too feels like an apt metaphor for writing.

Poetry might very well be a labor of love, but it is not an active labor—we cannot push our poems out.

Instead, we must let them incubate—*churn around below the threshold of consciousness*, as Mihaly Csikszentmihalyi writes—while simultaneously guarding and nurturing them as they develop, until they are too restless for the brittle containers of our design, until they are itching to break free and chip their way out.

And what a delicate delight then to watch these miraculous little things waddle away from us as we pray from the depths of our beings that they survive the cold of this world on their own.

Child's Play

I LIKE TO PLAY with my poems the way I play with my daughters. We invent elaborate games with ever-shifting rules. We take *familiar objects*, and invoking Shelley, treat them *as if they were not familiar*. When we wrestle, it almost looks like we're dancing.

The problem, though, is that other poems—poems I've never even read before—love to run over and join in on the fun, trying to grab my thumb or pull the glasses off my face. And before I know it, I'm surrounded by a pack of little rough drafts all wanting to play *slappy slappy*.

Not all poets appreciate it when you play with their poems in this way. They think poems should be seen and not heard, and they look at you disapprovingly when they notice their poems are suddenly barefoot and wild.

And not all poems like to engage with poets they don't know either—ask them something as innocent as their title, and they'll shoot you the stink eye.

Better that, though, than the poem that's licked all the frosting off its cupcake, then can't quite manage its sugar high— that equates being on the verge of a meltdown with the ecstatic transcendence of a creative breakthrough.

No, my favorite poems to play with are the ones that almost seem like they'd prefer to play by themselves. You have to earn their trust before they let you into their world. They would dance the whole night through if they weren't so wary of drawing attention to themselves.

And ever since I became a poet myself and realized just how much work it is to take care of poems—how they keep you up late at night, then wake you up early in the morning—I've come to truly appreciate what it means to play with other people's poems.

How freeing it is to go to someone else's house and rile their poems up, then give them back at the end of the night without having to worry about how you're going to settle them back down or wrangle them into their pajamas.

What a delight, too, to watch your poems play with other poets—to realize that you can never fully know a poem, to suddenly see it with fresh eyes.

And even though it's always so much easier when your poems fall asleep on the car ride home so you can listen to the second half of the game, you almost understand what Yeats means—as you listen to your poems go on and on now about the glow of the moon—when he says that *the world is full of magic things, patiently waiting for our senses to grow sharper.*

The Challenge of
Finding the Right Title

IN THE FIRST creative writing class I ever took, we workshopped a peer's story called *Tidal.*

I wrote a long critique of the piece, focusing on its ebb and flow and how its two references to the sea served as a motif for the stormy relationship between the two main characters.

It wasn't until I was sharing my interpretation aloud in class and referred to its self-referential title—*Tidal*—that I caught on to the joke. I felt duped and thrilled at the same time.

Whenever I find myself stuck in the middle of a poem, these days, I like to create a new file and make a long list of alternative titles—something I stole from Hemingway.

As unsettling as this can be, I love how it forces me to take my current draft and look for undercurrents, to imagine and reimagine what the piece might ultimately be about.

When my older daughter was younger, she came to us one night and asked if we could start calling her by a new name—Bevil.

When we agreed, it opened the floodgates, and before we knew it, her name had ballooned to Bevil-Red-Green-White-Green-and-Blue-Bugaboo-Rapper.

That didn't stick for long, of course, but she reveled in the freedom to reject the original name that we had forced upon her.

I like it when my poems feel that kind of freedom—when they grumble about self-determination and free will.

When my first book of poems, which focused on my time as a Peace Corps volunteer in Zimbabwe, was originally accepted for publication, I had called it *Close to Closure*. I liked the play between those two similar-sounding words and how they seemed to suggest that we never really move on from our pasts.

But a few months before it came out, a former mentor recommended the title *Strange Borderlands* instead. And suddenly the entire collection felt a little less sure of itself, more in touch with its tensions than intentions, and therefore more open to possibilities.

It reminds me of the way that my older daughter is always asking about what other names we considered for her before she was born, wondering what her life would have been like as an Alma or Maya or Oscar.

I like to revise my poems and stories until they have that kind of existential angst.

The challenge, I think, is figuring out how to construct meaning without constricting it, how to use the title to not only *capture* the essence of a poem but to *free* it.

Adventures in Screenwriting

DESPITE THE FACT that I don't own a TV, don't subscribe to Netflix, haven't been to a movie theater in years, and wouldn't know a slug line if it slugged me in the face, I decided to add a screenwriting unit to my creative writing class this past year.

To prepare, I spent the summer working on my own original screenplay—not only would this teach me a little something about the genre, I thought, but if I happened to pen a big hit, I just might never have to cover lunch duty again.

As a poet, I have very little experience writing dialogue or plotting stories into three acts. Although this made the writing process frustrating at times, it offered me many insights into the emotional challenges that my students—who are often writing creatively for the first time—tend to face.

I have tried to describe, here, the messy evolution of my screenplay and how it's changed my approach to teaching creative writing.

Writing the Screenplay:

Draft 1: Transformations

My first idea involved a character that feels lost in the modern world until he starts helping out at a funeral home. I was particularly interested in dramatizing an inner transformation through motifs and spent a week meticulously plotting the story out and storyboarding many of the scenes.

But when I actually started to write the screenplay, I ran into a familiar problem: my characters, much like my daughters, weren't actually interested in doing what I wanted them to do. I had planned their lives before I had taken the time to get to know them, and I soon realized that I would need to start over with a new premise and new process.

Draft 2: Are We Here Yet?

A few days later, I ran into a former student who had recently graduated from college and was struggling to figure out whether to accept a job offer or to spend the summer traveling abroad. She asked me for my advice. I asked her if she wanted to be the main character in my screenplay.

I started wondering what would happen if people didn't actually have to make big choices. What if my character could implant part of her soul into a pod and then send that pod abroad while she started her career? Would this solve my character's problem, I wondered, or simply create new ones?

After working with this sci-fi premise for a little over a week and discussing it with everyone I knew, I was asked by a screenwriter friend if I understood the whole budget aspect of films. *What do you mean?* I asked. *If you set ten minutes of your film abroad,* he told me, *you add $100,000 to your budget.*

And I realized that I was still writing with the freedom of a poet rather than attending to the realities of this new genre.

Draft 3: The Fad of the Land

The next day, I was at the farmer's market with my daughters when I saw a sign for Paleo Cookies. Paleo cookies? I thought. What Paleolithic ancestor ate vegan chocolate chip cookies sweetened with agave nectar?

I decided to start over entirely and write a comedy about two rival groups—the Paleos and the Kaleos—at a farmer's market.

I knew right away that this was a dumb idea, knew that I was writing a skit and not a feature-length film. But sometimes pursuing a dumb idea is an essential part of the creative process. It pressures us into a minor existential crisis, forces us to step back and reconsider our connection to our work.

And as I was thinking about why people would want to return to the traditional diets of our ancestors, I started contemplating my own relationship to the modern world, how the experiences that have felt most transformative to me—serving as a Peace Corps volunteer and becoming a father—both involved a return to simpler ways of living.

Draft 4: Vicarious 1

All of a sudden, I started to see some connections and patterns in my drafts and realized that what I really wanted to explore was this: in what ways do modern technological advances in this world help us feel more fulfilled? In what ways do they only exacerbate our loneliness?

I decided, then, to return to my previous sci-fi premise. My next draft was called *Vicarious* and was about a woman trying to save her family's pod service company from being sold to a hedonistic rival group.

This draft seemed to be going quite swimmingly: I felt deeply connected to the existential anxiety of my characters and had written half the screenplay when I realized that although I'd surrounded my protagonist with all sorts of interesting, quirky, and troubled characters, she was primarily a witness to the world around her—no struggles, desires, or conflicts of her own—and therefore no potential for an interesting arc.

I was disappointed that I was going to have to start over again. But I knew, too, that a heightened awareness of problems in a creative work is always a healthy sign.

Draft 5: Vicarious 2

So after three weeks of getting to know my main character, I decided to get rid of her. I kept the sci-fi premise but chose one of my minor characters to be my new protagonist—someone who uses her pod (now called Vikes) to evade and escape—and someone with the desire to change, as well. Finally, I had both a plot and a main character with potential, and the first twenty pages of the screenplay flew out of me in a few mornings.

The only problem now was that summer was over.

Some Takeaways:

I WENT INTO this project thinking that it would teach me the craft of screenwriting. And in many ways, it did. But the real question that emerged for me was this: How do we help students embrace the incredibly messy process of creative work?

You Say Revise, I Say Revive

It took me five different story treatments and well over two hundred pages of writing to net the first act of a screenplay. Yet each attempt was a better failure than the previous one. And that's not just because I'm a really bad screenwriter—every poem I've ever published has a hundred pages of failed drafts behind it.

And yet something that felt like such a natural part of the process to me—starting over—was something that my students always seemed to resist.

One strategy that I tried out this year was having my students write vision statements after they completed their first drafts. My job, I told them, was not to evaluate what they wrote based on my subjective tastes, but rather, it was to help them figure out how to write the best version of the story that they wanted to write.

One student, for example, had written a ten-page screenplay about the fallout between three friends after two of them begin dating. In her first draft, she followed the arc of the character that became the third wheel. But in her vision statement, she wrote that she was interested in exploring what it means to follow your heart even if it hurts someone else.

When we sat down to conference and recognized this disconnect, it was like a split-screen scene out of *Annie Hall.*

> *Now you just have to switch main characters and rewrite the story*, I said.
> *Now I have to switch main characters and rewrite the story??!!* she said.

Once she accepted this, she produced a much more realized draft. And I realized how important it is to build enough time into my units for deep revisions, to teach students the difference between finding material and shaping material, and to convince them that starting over is not a step backward but a step forward in a better direction.

Breaking Those Seas Frozen Inside Our Soul

But if I was going to ask my students to commit to deep revisions, I needed to help them think of their *work*, as Frost writes, as *play for mortal stakes.*

Another student, for example, turned in a first draft that was fifteen pages long and followed eleven different characters. When we sat down to conference, I suggested that she, umm, perhaps, choose one or two characters to focus on.

I can't, she said.

Why not? I asked.

I can't decide on which one, she said.

And then suddenly she was on the verge of tears, talking about the college process and having to decide between theater and field hockey, and these two very different boys whom she *kinda liked*, and how she never really knows what to do, and how her plot (or total lack thereof) was just one more example of her inability to ever make a decision about anything.

After depleting our class's PTO-sponsored box of tissues, we stepped back and realized that maybe what she really needed to do was transfer her own personal struggles onto her characters and let them manage.

She wrote twenty brilliant new pages over the weekend, following the story of an indecisive young actor struggling to decide whether to accept a role in a movie in which he would have to appear nude.

When we first sat down to conference, I had thought that my student needed help understanding the art of rising action; it turned out that she just needed to find a theme that she cared deeply about.

Putting My Grades Where My Mouth Is

If I wanted my students to embrace the messiness of the creative process, I needed to shift how I was grading them and put much more weight on their process, learning, and habits of mind.

I had one student, for example, who decided to adapt his favorite sci-fi book into a screenplay. His final product was pretty good, but it wasn't until I read his reflection—where he documented the struggles of his process—that I was truly able to see just how much he had learned. Here is a paragraph from his reflection:

> I began with the main events that I knew I wanted to transfer from the book to my screenplay and wrote them down on a time line. I then got more and more specific, choosing what events I wanted to translate, and ordering them in a way that both made sense and followed the three-act structure that movies so often do (in a book, for example, climaxes are not built up toward as dramatically as in a movie). This turned out to spawn a sort of liar's paradox, because whether a specific event could be included often depended on if there was a place for it, but where an event was to go often depended on whether another event could be included. In addition, the interwoven subplots and their subtle interactions with the main plot made the process somewhat like that of putting together a jigsaw puzzle made of shape-shifting pieces.

In creative projects, our learning is often inversely related to our success. My best students weren't necessarily the ones who were producing the most polished pieces—they were the ones coming away from their experiences with the most nuanced understanding of the challenges they had faced.

Conclusion:

SLOGGING THROUGH my own screenplay made me realize that while I was offering students many opportunities to be creative, I wasn't really teaching them how to be creative. I was showing them what good writing (the noun) looked like, but I wasn't teaching them what good writing (the verb) looked like.

Too often, I was offering students neat packages of learning with a focus on product over process: *here is some content, here are some skills, here is an assignment that will measure your learning.*

But the creative process typically looks more like this: *here is a brilliant idea that you will soon have to abandon, here is a heartbreaking setback, here is a minor epiphany in the middle of the night.*

Just this morning, I received the following email from one of my students on the verge of completing her first draft of a twenty-page screenplay.

> I just woke up in the middle of the night (it's 3:25 a.m.) and realized I'm not really passionate about my story. I think it strayed way too far from what I originally wanted to accomplish because looking back that goal was a little too big and overwhelming. So now it's turned into something completely different that I barely have any personal connection to. So, I'm kind of freaking out here. I want to rewrite it, but I'm worried it's too late. What should I do? Ahhhh!!!

And as messed up as this sounds, I almost cried tears of joy.

Teaching craft is essential. But if I want my students to think of writing as a lifelong apprenticeship, what I really need is to teach them to embrace the spirit of what Beckett means when he writes, *Ever tried. Ever failed. No matter. Try again. Fail again. Fail better.*

The Shape of a Story

V ONNEGUT WROTE his master's thesis on the theory that a computer is capable of graphing every possible story with good and ill fortune on the y-axis and time on the x-axis.

He believed that novels were ultimately about how characters get into and out of trouble and that plots—no matter how varied their premises—could be represented by a mere handful of simple shapes.

My four-year-old, on the other hand, like so many post-postmodernists of her generation, is interested in subverting literary conventions and inventing new ways to tell stories.

Some days, she'll call her imaginary friends on her toy phone and go on and on and on and on about her day—her stories a marriage of litany and tangents, like a cross between Whitman's catalogs and David Foster Wallace's footnotes.

Other days, she has no patience for steady arcs or logical discourse. She believes in escalation, and she believes in it now.

How about we put away those markers and take a bath? I'll say.

How about I dead your brain? she'll respond.

But while conversations with my four-year-old are entirely unpredictable, I've been worried lately that too many of my own poems could be graphed into the exact same shape.

I begin by pursuing one idea, and as soon as I've figured something out, I feel the need to reverse directions—consider the opposite of what I just said—until that too needs an opposing consideration. And before I know it, I've snaked my way up and down some mountain.

Not that there's anything wrong with switchbacks, but you can only take the same path so many times until you stop paying close attention, until the process is more about execution than exploration.

And when you focus too much on execution, you end up with dead poems.

The understanding of whether an experience is a linear sequence or a constellation raying out from and into a central focus or axis, for instance, is discoverable only in the work, not before it, writes Denise Levertov in her essay, "Some Notes on Organic Form."

Last night, my daughters and I were building a tower out of Magna-Tiles when I accidentally knocked half of it down.

I immediately started rebuilding it back into the exact same shape when my four-year-old stopped me and said, *Wait. Now it kind of looks like a spider-robot-monkey.* And suddenly, we were playing an entirely new game.

That's always both the scariest and most exciting moment of composition for me.

It's OK to know where we're going when we start a poem, I've learned, as long as we allow ourselves to shift directions during the writing process. Because no matter how well conceived our original idea is, something always collapses. But if we can weather the anxiety of starting over—think of it not as revising but as reenvisioning—we sometimes witness shape transcending into form.

Yet Another Reason
Not to Marry a Poet

I<small>T'S BEEN TOO LONG</small> since my wife and I have gone out on a date—found time to be alone with just one another and reconnect as a couple—but when the host seats us beside a giant aquatic tank, I am almost disappointed that our daughters aren't here with us to watch all these striped and spotted fish dart past the floating mermaids and over the sunken treasure chests.

It all feels so whimsical until I notice that directly across from the tank is the sushi bar where two uniformed men are turning slaughter into art. I am about to mention the cruel irony of this when the waitress appears.

My wife and I both order big bowls of noodle soup, and after the waitress leaves, we hold hands across the table, appreciating this rare opportunity to simply be present with one another.

Except I can't stop thinking about those fish—swimming so obliviously in their tank, unaware of the world beyond all that flimsy plastic décor—and how this has to be a metaphor for something.

My wife asks me if I have any hopes for the upcoming vacation, but even as I start to talk about how nice it will be to just have some time to slow down and reconnect as a family, to live in the here and now, my mind is like a third wheel and keeps wandering back to when I was a Peace Corps volunteer and would make jerky by hanging thin strips of goat from the clotheslines to dry in the hot sun, and how all the other goats would gather around and jump up and try to lick the dripping meat, not knowing that it was their dead brother that they were trying to eat.

That always made me so sad—even sadder than killing the goats in the first place—and is probably what led me to giving up meat for good.

The waitress brings out our soup, and my wife and I start slurping away, amazed at how much easier it is to eat dinner when there isn't a little person sitting next to you demanding that you pick out any flecks of orange that might have accidentally made their way onto their plate.

The soup is delicious, and we eat slowly, partly because it's so hot, partly to savor the varied flavors.

I ask my wife if she'd ever want to travel somewhere during one of our short winter breaks, and she tells me about how her family used to go down to Florida when she was a kid and how sometimes her parents would bring a babysitter along so that even the adults could feel like they were on vacation.

She looks so happy as she tells me about the shells that she and her sister used to collect, and I am about to suggest that we spend our credit card points on a family trip when the waitress walks by with a tray of sushi.

The colors are so strikingly beautiful that it is hard to believe that I am looking at dead animals.

I start thinking about the open markets in Marrakesh where the stalls were lined with sheep heads and how shop owners used to crack those heads open with hammers and scoop out the brains and put them in clear plastic bags—how the violence of meat wasn't hidden there, how the packaging didn't try to pretend that it was something different than what it was.

I look down and realize that I am almost finished with my soup and that our date is almost over, and I am suddenly overcome with regret.

I want to tell my wife how beautiful she looks tonight, how lucky I am that she ever agreed to marry me. I want to confess that every morning, I wake up, and the very first thing that I do is kiss her on the cheek—how even in sleep, she is so radiant—and although I'm just getting up to write in the next room, to wander the winding neighborhoods of my mind, every time I leave her, I feel like that guy in the James Wright poem who looks up at the sky from his hammock and realizes that he has wasted his life.

I am about to tell her all of this when it hits me that this might be the metaphor that I was looking for earlier—my thoughts are those darting exotic fish, and my head is the giant tank that they are trapped in.

And even though I know that this comparison is incomplete, a first and all-too-obvious attempt that doesn't even take into account what the sushi bar might represent, I can barely wait to get home now so that I can write all these ideas down before they swim away forever.

The Power of Disruption

L AST NIGHT, I was brushing my teeth when I noticed a pair of socks in the toilet.

Why are your socks in the toilet? I asked my four-year-old.

Mama told me to put them away in my drawer, she said.

So how did they end up in the toilet? I asked.

Didn't feel like putting them away in my drawer, she said.

And although I wasn't in the mood to put on a pair of rubber gloves and fish my four-year-old's socks out of the toilet, I've come to appreciate that such disruptions are at the heart of every good story.

At its most basic level, a disruption is what flings a piece of writing forward.

We meet a character going about life in the most mundane of ways when, *Wham!*, along comes some inciting incident to transform them into a protagonist. Or said protagonist is on a clear path toward a goal until, *Bam!*, some obstacle forces them to distinguish between what they want and what they need.

Poems—especially poems that work their way through an argument (even if it's a *quarrel*, as Auden said, *with ourselves*)— also thrive on disruptions.

The sonnet, of course, is known for dramatically shifting directions with a *volta* between its octave and sestet, but such shifts are essential to the movement of many contemporary poems as they snake their way through paradoxical ideas, each turn inciting a new insight.

The problem, though, is that it can be hard to find the right-sized disruption.

Too often, when composing a piece, we find ourselves encountering an *interruption*, an unexpected problem that gives us slight pause before we continue on our merry way.

The story or poem knows where it's going from the get-go, and, although it slows down to overcome an obstacle or consider a contradiction, it's like trying to convince your uncle that climate change isn't fake news—he might let you speak your piece, but you're not really changing his mind.

At other times, we find *disruption*'s postmodern cousins—*discontinuity* and *discombobulation*—knocking at our door.

They zoom around our tidy stanzas like Thing One and Thing Two, unsettle us with such existential anxiety that afterward we no longer trust language's ability to convey the simplest of truths, because language itself is about as stable as a goldfish jar on top of a rake.

And because too many evenings these days offer a *Cat in the Hat* kind of balancing act—unpacking the day's lunches with one hand while making tomorrow's lunches with the other—I often find myself desperately seeking routine and order.

But on my better days, I'm able to recognize the beauty of chaos, watch my four-year-old dump an entire tray of silverware into the bath so she can host a royal feast for her rubber duckies—and see not the wake of destruction but the wakefulness of disruption.

The Trouble with Transitions

M Y DAUGHTERS were supposed to be getting ready for bed when I walked into their room and found my four-year-old naked, kneeling on all fours with her butt in the air, her older sister slapping her bottom.

What are you doing? I asked.

Playing the drums, my older daughter said.

And although part of me was relieved to see my four-year-old finally using her butt for something other than a wind instrument, I immediately stopped the show and escorted her to the shower.

It got me thinking, though, about the difficulty of transitions in both parenting and writing.

I am often amazed by how hard it is to get my daughters into the shower, and then once they're in the shower, how hard it is to get them out—and this feels eerily similar to the challenge of making my way from one stanza or paragraph to the next.

More often than not, this is a result of how I go about putting a draft together in the first place—which typically involves a series of false starts and frenzied free-writes, frantic late-night calls to my muse and failed attempts at remembering the epiphany I had in the middle of the night.

Before I know it, I've amassed a collection of undercurrents and overhauls that refuse to be shaped into a coherent narrative.

At best, the writing process becomes a matter of culling

through draft after draft after draft, then pulling my favorite passages and trying to create passageways.

Every finished piece of writing only seems seamless.

What makes transitions particularly difficult for me, though, is that despite my love of psychic shifts, I get so easily overwhelmed by contradictions.

I wonder if this is what makes transitions hard for my daughters as well—they're rocking out to *Hairspray* in their bedroom, singing at the top of their lungs about how no one can *stop the music*, how no one can *stop the beat*, and then suddenly I barge in, stop both the music *and* the beat, and demand that they start their bedtime routines.

What else is there to do—when faced with the dizzying disconnects of this world—but find a butt and start drumming, and try to remember, as Roxane Gay writes, that *nothing makes sense but still, somehow, there is a rhythm.*

Minor Moves, Major Impacts

A FEW YEARS AGO, I was reading the *American Poetry Review* when I came across the following gem by Beth Ann Fennelly.

Practical

Bought a bag of frozen peas to numb my husband's sore testicles after his vasectomy.

That night I cooked pea soup.

I loved how Fennelly accomplished so much in such a small space—how this tiny poem offered us such a humorous but poignant glimpse into a marriage—and it quickly became one of my favorite texts to use in my creative writing classes.

So I was surprised this morning to come across a slightly revised version of the piece in her wonderful book, *Heating & Cooling*. The revised piece reads like this:

Married Love, IV

Morning: bought a bag of frozen peas to numb my husband's sore testicles after his vasectomy.

Evening: added thawed peas to our carbonara.

A piece of this size doesn't give one much room to work with in terms of revisions. But poets are used to working with tweezers, and by examining the slight revisions that she did make, I think that we can better understand how minor moves can have major impacts.

First, Fennelly changed the title from "Practical" to "Married Love, IV."

Maybe it's just the image of seeing titles on top of poems, but whenever I change one, it always feels as though I am giving the poem a haircut. Sometimes it's just a trim to clean things up a bit, and sometimes it's an entirely new hairstyle.

This poem clearly went to one of those fancy salons because the new title signifies that no longer is this piece just about the quirky pragmatism of the speaker; it is now part of a larger thematic sequence, bouncing off the other "Married Love" entries to explore the complex layers of what love looks like twenty years into a marriage.

Second, Fennelly adds *Morning:* and *Evening:* at the beginning of each sentence. This doesn't change the time line of the two events; it simply heightens the tension between them. The two stanzas are no longer just juxtaposed; they are now tightly arranged.

It reminds me of when my wife breaks out the label maker and suddenly starts reorganizing one of our closets, harnessing the natural energy of our toiletries to establish peace, harmony, and balance.

But this is the essence of poetry—attending to tensions in pattern and form, rhythm and cadences. *The most compelling ideas for me*, writes Danielle Legros Georges, *come from the marriage of seemingly disparate notions*, and Fennelly's revision is an example of parallel structure at its finest, using syntactic similarities to highlight semantic differences.

Third, while the first sentence essentially stays the same, Fennelly changes a single detail in the second sentence. Pea soup works under the title, "Practical," but it's too mundane for "Married Love." Carbonara, on the other hand, takes some effort to make—hints at a more romantic dinner—and thus contrasts even more strongly with the previous sentence.

And there is something about the visual image of a wrinkly, thawed pea—rather than the ones blended into a soup—that makes it harder to forget where that bag had been resting all morning.

Poets specialize in the art of compression—saying as much as they can in as few words as possible—and Fennelly's close attention to language provides us with a glimpse of how even the slightest of revisions can lead to great transformations.

The Secret to a Great Arc

*M*AKE YOUR CHARACTERS *want something right away,* writes Vonnegut, *even if it's only a glass of water.* And as soon as we pick my four-year-old up from preschool and strap her into her car seat, she tells us that she is thirsty.

But a narrative, at its most basic level, is driven by the relationship between what a character wants and the obstacles in the way, and it just so happens that my daughter's water bottle is empty.

Can I have some of your water? my four-year-old asks.

But even she must know—from every book that we've ever read to her—that a character can't reach a goal without a little resistance, because the dramatic arc of a story relies on the heightening tension between hope and disappointment.

And while both my wife and I have water to share, I'm sick with a cold, and my wife has added electrolytes to hers that, unfortunately, contain caffeine.

We could stop at a store, my four-year-old suggests. And lo and behold, a Walgreens appears just ahead to our left.

However, while stopping to buy bottled water would certainly expedite our path to a climax, a good story must find ways to complicate the inner journey of the protagonist.

And when I explain to my four-year-old that we can't stop because we are already late to pick her older sister up, I can sense both the target and intensity of her frustration beginning to shift.

My wife tries to distract her by sharing that she once learned that should you ever find yourself stranded in the desert, you could suck on a stone because they absorb moisture from the air.

But I immediately object to this, not simply because I'm pretty sure that I remember Dr. Spock saying something about not letting your kids suck on rocks in the car, but because giving her a rock to suck on would provide her with a deus ex machina.

No, I say, *the change must come from within.*

I remind my four-year-old of Rumi's quote about seeking *not water, but thirst*, but she has no patience for Sufi mysticism and begins grunting and kicking the back of my car seat.

Normally, this would bother me. But I know that sometimes a character has to hit rock bottom in order to realize that they need to undergo some sort of personal transformation if they want to reach their goal.

And yet, the more my daughter digs her heels into my seat, the more I begin to worry that in my four-year-old's mind— where everything is a competition—she is equating *personal transformation* with *losing*.

And the louder she screams, the more I begin to wonder if I've been tracing the wrong character's arc—that maybe this isn't the story of a young girl on a quest for water but the story of a middle-aged man who finally learns to stop thinking of his children's greatest struggles and desires as metaphors for the creative process.

I look back at my daughter, whose face is covered in tears, and I suddenly grok her pain—she is tired and strapped in and thirsty—and I remember my own childhood, when I'd spend all day suffering small humiliations on the playground, then wait until I got home to explode on the people who were contracted by ancient law to forgive me.

Poets traffic in awareness, writes Alan Shapiro, and each whack to the back of my seat registers like a Zen master's stick until I am climactically aware of my daughter's pain.

I hit the gas and speed down the back roads until we finally make it to my older daughter's school, jump out of the car, and rush my four-year-old to the nearest water fountain so that she might quench her unbearable thirst.

But my four-year-old just looks up at that perfect arc of water and announces that she's not thirsty anymore, then takes off skipping down the hallway.

Only then does the story feel complete. Only then do I sense an ending that offers us both closure and the reminder that we live, as I once heard Lorrie Moore say, in a *constant state of nonarrival.*

In Praise of the Colon

THE COLON might be the least poetic punctuation mark of all. It serves the same rhetorical purposes as the em dash, but the em dash looks like a bridge between ideas. The colon looks like a gutted ellipsis rising from the grave.

And yet, there have been a few poets who've used the colon extensively in their poems. Take A. R. Ammons, for example. David Lehman writes of Ammon's usage: *The colon permits him to stress the linkage between clauses and to postpone closure indefinitely.*

However, Ammons uses colons so indiscriminately in his poems that it can be hard to infer a singular meaning—like some prankster who has littered the neighborhood with yield signs.

No ideas but in things, writes William Carlos Williams, and I like the way that the colon occupies the space between the idea and the thing, between the concept and the illustration of the concept. It is the mark of expectation, the need for further nuance, which strikes me as the guiding spirit of all good poems.

And yet, to go back to Ammons, the colon does make us wonder if poems ever *click like a closing box*, the way Yeats describes it, or if they are *only abandoned*, as Paul Valéry says.

After all, we also use the colon after an independent clause—in place of a period—the complete sentence that's not really a complete sentence. It reminds me of my nightly argument with my older daughter about whether she's actually finished practicing piano.

In dramatic writing, the colon signifies the space between the person and what the person says—and for me, writing is often about figuring out how to shift into a voice, how to transition from my person into my persona.

Because colon cancer runs in my family, I spent last weekend preparing for my first colonoscopy, which entailed guzzling a half gallon of liquid laxatives, then sleeping upstairs so as not to disturb the rest of my family.

Though it was all worth it just to hear my younger daughter whisper to her friend this morning: *Do you want to go upstairs and see where my daddy does his diarrhea?* And then to see my daughter's friend offer such an enthusiastic response.

Still, of all the colon's uses, it's the *PS:* that's my favorite—that sense of wanting to go on forever.

The way my older daughter kept calling me back to her room last night after I tucked her in to ask: *But what happens to us after we die?*

How to Deal with Setbacks
in the Creative Process

I WAS COOKING DINNER when my five-year-old crawled on over to me. *Googoo, gaga*, she said, raising her arms up in the air. I picked her up and patted her back until she burped.

Now that kindergarten is around the corner, my daughter loves to pretend that she's a baby—wants to be spoon-fed at dinner and asks to be rocked to sleep.

Her regressions would be much more worrisome if I didn't experience the same process with every single poem I've ever written.

Just last week, I decided to make some final edits to a poem that I was preparing to send out—wanted to fine-tune an image and rework the rhythm of a line. But a little minor tweaking soon turned into some heavy pruning, and before I knew it, my poem looked like a plundered village.

I think that I had suddenly felt the pressure of submission and tried to guard the poem from every vicious critique of an imagined editor who would immediately recognize all its flaws. By the next morning, I was ready to give up on the poem altogether and file it away in my drawer of failed poems.

It wasn't until I was talking with an actress friend of mine later in the week that I was able to see my own process with some clarity and perspective.

My friend had just finished a dress rehearsal for a play that was set to open in a few days, and so much had gone wrong—missed cues, misplaced props, injuries from a botched costume change—that she worried the director was going to cancel the show.

But opening night went fabulously, of course, and it reminded me that setbacks are a natural and necessary part of the process— they refocus you and remind you of what's at stake. And when I returned to my poem the following morning, the revisions just kind of flowed out of me with grace and ease.

Oftentimes, in creative work, we reach a point in the path where we can no longer go forward unless we make some great leap. And so, we turn around—not to retreat to our cars but to get a running start, create enough momentum to clear the crevasse, and make it to the other side where a stunning view awaits.

At least, that is what I tell myself when my five-year-old finds some old Elmo diapers in her closet and asks if she can try one on.

Of course, I say, trying to convince myself that there's no need to check in with her pediatrician—she's just getting a really, *really* big running start as she prepares for the big leap to kindergarten.

Why Finding the Right Image Can Be So Challenging

I PLACE THE SIX-PACK of beer on the counter.

The clerk looks up at me, then down at the beer, then back up at me, then leans in and says, *I thought I was gonna have to ID you when you first walked in, but now that you're up close, I can see all the gray hairs on your head.*

I'm not sure whether to be flattered that he thinks I look twenty years younger than I actually am or upset that he's noticed that I am starting to go gray.

Although, after I get home and examine my head in the mirror, I realize that there is something about the word *gray* that feels off—as though it is too generic a word to capture the intricate blending of complementing colors sprouting from my head.

Later at dinner, I ask my wife and daughters if they will help me find a more evocative, surprising, and accurate description of my hair.

My wife suggests that my head looks like the love child of a panda and a koala bear, but my seven-year-old seems downright offended that my wife would compare me to animals that are so adorably cute.

What about storm clouds? I offer. *Or campfire smoke?*

Both of these images seem somewhat accurate in terms of color, and I like that they speak to the impending dangers of a midlife crisis. But there is something too billowy about their presence. The grays on my head aren't about to be blown away, and I need an image that is more accurately textured.

Salt and pepper, my wife suggests.

That one's familiar, of course, and I kind of like it. But it feels imprecise. My hair is mostly the color of pepper with a little dash of salt mixed in. *Pepper and salt* would be more accurate, but even then, the secondary meaning of the word *pepper* seems to suggest that it is the black *peppered* about.

Part of the challenge is that I want to find an image that speaks to the rapid changes of aging. For forty years, I have enjoyed thickly settled jet-black hair, and now all of a sudden, it is as though the top of my head is being gentrified—all these little white clusters popping up all over the place.

I think your hair is beautiful, says my five-year-old. *Like the color of a princess's poop.*

This comparison is certainly surprising, evocative, and tonally complex, but unless that princess has been taking iron supplements, it is also totally inaccurate. And yet, I appreciate the absurdity of my five-year-old's suggestion and how it frees my mind to traverse the surreal.

It's never easy coming up with an image that works on both a literal and figurative level, and I am looking for something that is visually accurate but also reflective of my resistance to the fact that my youthfulness is beginning to fade.

My hair's not gray, I suddenly say. *It's Dorian Gray.*

My daughters look at me like I am an idiot, and even though there isn't anything visual about that line, there is something about the mixture of playfulness and seriousness that I like.

I've always considered myself young at heart, but now my body is starting to tell a different story.

And later, when I sneak into the bathroom and use tweezers to pluck a white hair or three, I can't help but recognize what feels like an ancient literary pull, a deep and existential tug.

What to Expect
When You're Expectorating

M Y FIVE-YEAR-OLD is into spitting these days. Not the nasty huck-a-loogie-over-a-rail kind of spitting but the motorboat-your-lips-and-spray-saliva-all-over-the-place kind of spitting.

I find the whole thing kind of funny until she hoses me in the face for saying no to potato chips for breakfast. Then, I sit her down and explain that big kids use words when they are upset and that spitting on someone else is never ever OK.

But Papa, she says, *that's my thing.*

I want to explain to her that five-year-olds are too young to have things and at best have phases that, with any luck, they quickly grow out of.

But there is something so strikingly unapologetic about her defense—as though spitting is her way of speaking her truth—that the writer in me suddenly wants a thing of my own.

After all, writers have always been celebrated for defying the conventional rules and trusting their own visions—e. e. cummings capitalizing on his refusal to capitalize, Dickinson transforming her dashed literary dreams into a rage of dashes. And now that we've entered the digital age, you need more than verbal precision and a heightened awareness of ambiguity to make it as a poet. It's all about building a brand and going viral, about transforming your thing into a style.

However, as soon as I start imagining what my thing might be, I immediately feel myself getting overwhelmed, worrying that I might not have a thing or that the things I do have aren't actually that interesting.

Maybe I'm just feeling defensive, but I start to wonder if it would be reductive to only allow ourselves a single thing. After all, *the purpose of poetry*, writes Czesław Miłosz, *is to remind us / how difficult it is to remain just one person.*

What if I had a plethora of things? I think to myself, and start making a list of all the various vices that I'd like to be able to get away with.

And yet, to be a poet is to write with the ear, and the cretic *that's my thing* sounds so much better than the choriamb *those are my things*, or the perfectly iambic *my things are in a constant state of flux.*

And so, I look at my list and start the process of elimination, and I realize that, of all the possible things that might be mine, it's probably my predilection for wordplay, my love for the lightness of language and weight of words, that has the most potential.

I feel like I'm finally ready to embrace this idea that we should all have a single thing that we can get away with when I look over at my five-year-old and see that she is spitting into a fan so that it sprays back into her own face. She is spitting and giggling, then spitting some more.

Surely, a better parent would step in and stop this nonsense right here and right now.

But I just sit back and watch her take such delight in the sensory pleasures of life and can't stop myself from thinking *that girl is my spitting image.*

It's no time for puns. But what can I do?

That's my thing.

Dissecting the Frog

WHEN MY OLDER DAUGHTER was three years old, her favorite joke went like this:

> Q: *What do you call a funny hill?*
> A: *Hilarious.*

In many ways, this had all the makings of a joke—it followed the question-answer form, offered a punch line that attempted a play on words—but psychologists often speak about the importance of incongruity in humor, and the comic effect here mostly stemmed from the gap between my daughter's understanding of a joke and our expectations.

Now that she's seven, her sense of humor has evolved, and her new favorite joke goes like this:

> Q: *What do you call a deer with no eyes?*
> A: *No-eyed-deer.*

This joke presents a different kind of incongruity, and there's something about the punch line that simultaneously delights and disturbs as the feigned innocence of what we first hear as *no idea* gives way to the troubling image of a mutilated doe.

But the joke isn't quite over; she follows it with this one:

Q: *What do you call a deer with no eyes and no legs?*
A: *Still no-eyed-deer.*

This joke always gets more of a groan than a laugh—maybe the image has grown too grotesque, maybe the punch line is too predictable. But it doesn't matter because this joke is merely a setup—yes, it raises the stakes by punning on two words and providing an even more disturbing image, but its primary purpose is to establish an expectation so that she can surprise us in the third act.

Just when we think we've figured out the formula, she breaks out this joke:

Q: *What do you call a fish with no eyes?*
A: *A fsh.*

This joke relies on incongruity as well, but it also taps into what psychologists refer to as *relief theory*—laughter as the release of pent-up nervous energy. Just as we've braced ourselves for even more dismemberment, the punch line reverses direction, and puns instead on the word *eye* and the letter *i.*

As simple as these jokes are, I think they illustrate some interesting ideas about narrative structure. We can see a similar framework at play in this much more troubling joke that I recently heard Devorah Baum tell in a discussion of her book, *The Jewish Joke.*

> *After Elie Wiesel dies, he goes to Heaven and has the chance*
> *to meet God.*

The opening line immediately makes us uncomfortable, as telling a joke about something as traumatic as the Holocaust pushes the boundaries of what humor theorists call *benign violation.*

"I'm not sure if this is appropriate," he says to God. "But I have a great Holocaust joke I'd like to tell you."

This second line is part of the setup, and its job is to raise the stakes and heighten the tension: not only is Wiesel in a joke about the Holocaust, but he is telling God a joke about the Holocaust.

"Go ahead," says God. So Elie Wiesel tells God his best Holocaust joke and God just looks at him stone-faced—not even the slightest smile.

This line begins to provide some relief—thank goodness that God is in the joke to offer us a moral center!

"Well," says Elie Wiesel, "I guess you had to be there."

The final line then reverses direction, and it's again the combination of relief and incongruity that creates the humor.

On the one hand, we are relieved that Wiesel is not the target of a joke, and the punch line offers us the chance to release that nervous energy. But there's also great discordance in that final line. *I guess you had to be there*—that familiar throwaway apology that we offer when our jokes fall flat—now serves as a profoundly troubling existential accusation. And it's the merging of these two incredibly incongruous tones and meanings that creates shock and humor.

Analyzing humor is like dissecting a frog, writes E. B. White. *Few people are interested and the frog dies of it.*

And while there's nothing funny about killing defenseless animals, surely there is somebody out there at this very moment trying to figure out how to turn a frog with no eyes, no legs, and no organs into the cleverest of punch lines.

How Writing Returns Us to Wonder

WE ARE in the CVS parking lot, waiting for my wife to finish some errands, when my five-year-old notices an inchworm on her car window and starts to panic.

It's OK, I say. *It's on the outside.*

I don't care, she screams. *Kill it!*

It will fly off when we start driving, I say.

No, my seven-year-old says from the other side of the car. *You have to save it.*

I don't really feel like getting up, but I also don't feel like listening to *The Greatest Showman* soundtrack yet again, so I get out of the car and try to pull the inchworm off the window.

There is a fine line between pulling an inchworm off a window and squishing its guts out, but I finally pluck it between my fingers, then look around until I spot a patch of green that I've somehow never noticed before.

I walk on over and flick my hand back and forth until it falls onto the grass. Except it doesn't fall—it dangles in midair, spinning like a trapeze artist from my hand—until I gently lower it and lay it down between a cigarette butt and a Skittles wrapper.

In a moment, I will return to the car and for the first time in a month, I will not beg my daughters to switch to a new CD. Instead, I will join them as they sing along to "Come Alive."

My wife will return from her errands, and I will not ask what took her so long; I will hold her hand and notice its warmth and the roughness of her calluses.

And then I will drive home and forget entirely about this moment—because who has time for transcendence when there are lunches to put away and dinners to make and laundry to wash and arguments to be had with your five-year-old about whether she needs to wear pants when she plays in the front yard.

Chances are I will not think about this inchworm ever again unless I wake up early the next morning and sit down at my desk and open my journal where I will write, aimlessly at first, describing the inchworm in plain and simple terms—its tiny hairs and translucent green, the way it arched and straightened toward the one purple flower in the lot—until the language begins to surprise me, and I find myself writing about the strength and delicacy of invisible threads, the challenge of applying just the right amount of pressure.

Soon, I will find myself writing about how hard it is, as we grow older, to feel the kind of fascination we felt as kids. I will look up the word *fascination* and learn that it comes from *fascinus*, meaning the *embodiment of the divine phallus*, and for the briefest of moments, I will even consider writing a poem about the inchworm as a tiny green divine phallic symbol.

I will remember Ross Gay saying that when we pay attention, we find ourselves *in the midst of an almost constant, if subtle, caretaking.*

I will think about how my five-year-old was scared and how my seven-year-old believes that all life is sacred, and I will see the words *scared* and *sacred* near one another and think there's a poem there too.

And although these journal entries will never really go anywhere, I will be so grateful that, for a few hours before the busyness of the day, I have this time to contemplate the world with a mixture of reverie and reverence.

Write What You Don't Know

MY FIVE-YEAR-OLD always protests whenever she sees me bring out my poetry bag—the briefcase I use when I go out for readings—knowing that I won't be home in time to tuck her in. But a few nights ago, upon seeing it in the corner of the living room, she pumped her fist in the air and announced: *Aww yeah! Bring out the videos and candy!*

I looked over at my wife, who was vigorously avoiding eye contact, and suddenly felt like I was a character in one of those children's books where all the magic happens behind the parent's back—though typically, in those books, it happens behind *both* parents' backs.

There was something, too, about my daughter's line that reminded me of a former writing teacher who used to tell us that *a poem doesn't start until it startles you.*

I don't think I really understood what he meant at the time, because when you're eighteen and jumping from one existential crisis to the next, it's not exactly hard to startle yourself. But now that I've settled into middle age, it often takes me much longer to shift into those deep exploratory states of mind.

I think this is why I like to get up so early to write while my dream mind is still active, and I am more *capable of being in uncertainties, mysteries,* [and] *doubts,* as Keats writes, *without any irritable reaching after fact and reason.*

I am more likely, then, to return to what Zen Buddhists call *beginner's mind*, more open to the spontaneity of composition, more willing to relinquish control and follow my words wherever they take me. And on my better days I find that parenting works in the same way—my daughters are constantly unsettling what I think I know about them.

The kids that I slather with sunscreen before camp are not the same kids that I greet with juice boxes in the afternoon. They have made and lost friends since I last saw them, taken great risks, and suffered small humiliations.

I never know—when they get into the car—if they're going to ask if we can stop for ice cream on our way home, or if they're going to ask, as my seven-year-old did yesterday afternoon, *How do babies even get in there in the first place?*

There's nothing wrong, of course, with the old dictum *write what you know*, but I also want my poems to be as bewildering and unpredictable as my children.

On the Shoulders of Giants

WHOEVER SAID there's no such thing as a free ride hasn't met my five-year-old.

Whenever it's time to walk home from the playground, she will start to deflate like a football in New England, will refuse to take another step forward until I hoist her over my head and onto my shoulders so that she can bounce up and down as we walk home, picking leaves off the trees or pretending that she's in a marching band and the side of my head is her drum.

I, on the other hand, have no choice but to suffer through her glory, my back tightening as she breaks out her favorite dance moves.

And none of the old women who coo as they walk by even notice me. All they see is an adorable little girl doing the floss dance and offering the queen's wave—as though she's just floating magically in the air.

I am convinced, of course, that this is a metaphor for the creative life.

Creative people combine playfulness and discipline, or responsibility and irresponsibility, writes Mihaly Csikszentmihalyi. *There is no question that a playfully light attitude is typical of creative individuals. But this playfulness doesn't go very far without its antithesis, a quality of doggedness, endurance, perseverance.*

I often see this play out in the relationship between Curious Me and Serious Me.

Curious Me is relentlessly interested in new ideas, pursues them like a dog that has just smelled the pee of another dog, like a toddler pulling every toy out of the bin.

Serious Me, on the other hand, spends half his time cleaning up all the sentence frags and half-finished ideas that Curious Me has left littered about.

There are some days when this relationship is a beautiful example of opposites attracting. After all, these paradoxical traits are essential, Csikszentmihalyi goes on to say, as *creative individuals . . . contain contradictory extremes; instead of being an "individual," each of them is a "multitude."*

But there are other days when our paradoxical traits do nothing but bicker, as though they're auditioning for yet another reboot of *The Odd Couple.*

Part of the problem is that Serious Me gets so frustrated by the clutter of messy ideas that he can't tolerate Curious Me's incessant desire to play.

But Curious Me also tends to take Serious Me for granted. On the rare occasion that she willingly agrees to leave the playground of ideas, she demands a pony ride home.

And if, God forbid, Serious Me ever has to slow down to stretch, Curious Me starts making snide comments—like my seven-year-old, who told me the other day, *You might look strong, but really you're just a big stew of dumplings.*

But writing a book is a long and arduous journey, and if Curious Me hopes to make it to the end, she needs to remember that *creative people,* as Csikszentmihalyi writes, *are well aware that they stand, in Newton's words, "on the shoulders of giants."*

The Secret of Gifted Writers

THERE IS AN EXIT off the Mass Pike in Cambridge where cars merge from so many lanes at once that driving feels like the physical manifestation of writer's block.

And although I tend to view such bottlenecks as the bane of urban living, my wife somehow always sees them as a blessing—an opportunity to slow down and notice the man on the median with a cup and cardboard sign, to model for our daughters what we mean when we tell them, *We're not obligated to complete the work, but neither are we free to ignore it.*

What often strikes me about my wife's generosity is that it isn't limited to the act of giving; she is also remarkably gracious when it comes to receiving gifts. My five-year-old will present her with some crumpled-up hot mess of scribbles, and my wife will swoon and immediately hang it on the fridge.

I am convinced that this trait—this openness to whatever gifts the world may bring—is essential to the creative process.

When I first started writing, I would often stare at the blinking cursor on the blank page waiting for inspiration, longing for some vision of *a stately pleasure-dome* to just flow out of me or for *three strange angels*, as D. H. Lawrence writes, to come *knocking at the door.*

Then the Muse would stop by and drop off some half-felt emotion or unformed idea or recurring dream that not even

Freud could make sense of, and I would find myself growing resentful—as though the Muse was Santa Claus, and I was the only Jewish writer in town.

But the more I write, the more I've come to recognize the importance of staying receptive to whatever the Muse throws our way.

Here's an image of some mouse droppings under the sink, she tells us. *And here's one of a diaper bundled so tight, it looks like a perfectly wrapped present.*

And yet, if we can find a space for these things in our imagination, they often lead us to new insights and unexpected connections.

A few days ago, my brother came over with a Beanie Boo—a little stuffed animal that you hook onto your backpack—for my older daughter. There are hundreds of these Beanie Boos out there, and my brother just happened to buy the very one that my daughter already owned.

When my seven-year-old realized this, she immediately ran into the other room, grabbed her Beanie Boo off her backpack, showed it to my brother, and then declared with the greatest of joy: *I've always wanted twins!*

It reminded me of the game that my wife and daughters sometimes play—where one person draws an incomplete figure on a piece of paper and then hands it to someone else to finish—how so much of art is about seeing the possibility in whatever stray marks come our way.

Mistress of the Middle

M Y FIVE-YEAR-OLD loves helping me make pickles—though at
the moment she is upset that I won't let her pour the boiling
water into the mason jars and jerks her hand away when I try to
help her chop the dill.

I tell her that she can be in charge of adding the cucumbers to
the brine while I wipe the counters and sweep the floor. She pretends
that each one is terrified of jumping into the pool and that she is
their coach, gently encouraging them in.

She finally finishes, and we tighten the lids and head outside
where my older daughter is riding her bike up and down the street. I
ask my five-year-old if she wants to ride her bike, but she tells me that
training wheels are boring and asks if we can play Wiffle ball instead.

But even Wiffle ball frustrates her today as she insists on using
the skinny yellow bat rather than Big Bertha.

After a dozen pitches or so, she asks me to bring out the sidewalk
chalk so that we can write our names on the driveway. We do this
for a good twenty minutes before she tells me that she's hungry, so
we head back inside and poke around the fridge—but she doesn't
like any of the choices and asks if she can have a pickle.

It takes three days, I tell her.

I just want to try one, she says. So, I take out a spear and cut it up.

It tastes like a wet and salty cucumber, she says. I try to explain
that that's what it *is*, but she gives me one of her looks.

I make sandwiches, and then we all get in the car to drive to
Cambridge and visit my baby nephew. Though now that he's turned

one, my younger daughter insists that we shouldn't use the word *baby* anymore.

I love watching my daughters play with their cousin. They hold his hands as he takes tentative steps across the floor, let him crawl all over them, don't get upset when he pulls their hair. They feed him strawberries, play endless rounds of peekaboo, even sing him a lullaby when it's time for us to leave.

We head home, and I'm about to start cooking when my five-year-old asks if she can have pickles for dinner.

I remind her that it takes three days and tell her that I'm making pasta with shakey cheese—her favorite—but she crosses her arms and tells me that she won't eat a single noodle, won't eat anything tonight other than a plateful of pickles.

I sit down next to her and try to explain that brine isn't just some sauce that flavors the cucumber but that the mason jar is kind of like a cocoon and it takes time for the cucumbers to transform into pickles.

I don't care, she screams, *I don't care*.

And I realize that we're not talking about pickles anymore.

I hold her in my lap, and she cradles into my arms, and I suddenly remember a game that I used to play as a kid that was actually called *pickle* and involved running back and forth between bases.

Some of my friends were masters of the middle: they would fake left then juke right, toy with the throwers until they could run right past the latter and slide into safety. But I always just ended up running in circles until I was too dizzy and tired to make my next move before one of the taggers could close in and shove me to the ground.

I'm about to tell this to my daughter when I see that she is on the verge of tears. So, I get up and take out a couple of spears and cut them into pieces. I can tell by her face that she doesn't like the taste or the texture.

But that's not going to stop her. She made them. And she's not going to wait any longer.

The Prose Poem as a Jew

NOT THAT LIFE was all that bad in France compared to the rest of Europe, but we came to America with dreams of making it new.

And in some ways, we did. The problem, though, was that to fit in you always felt this pressure to be something that you weren't.

There were these anthologies back then where all the short stories liked to hang out, and usually, there would be these rules about no poems allowed. But we could pass, at first, because technically we were prose. But then sometimes you'd be telling some story and everyone would just stare at you, and you kind of knew what they were thinking: *You might look like a paragraph, but you act like a poem.*

And whenever we'd try to make our way into some of the top literary journals, they'd pull us aside and say, *Look, it's nothing personal—some of my favorite passages are prose poems. But if we let one into our journal, who knows what would try to get in next.*

Once it became clear that we would never be fully accepted, we tried to go back to being poems.

But the poetry world had moved on—it was all about the line now. *They taste good to her / They taste good / to her. They taste / good to her* etc., etc.

Look, we would say, *we may not have line breaks, but we are as broken as any of you.*

But poems can be so pretentious—they'll refer to you as a hybrid to your face but call you lowbred behind your back.

So, what else could we do but form our own anthologies? And that was kind of empowering at first. But even within our tiny insular community, there seemed to be this split: the surrealists wanted new ways to wander the unconscious while the narratives were content to be lyrically compressed.

Soon, it felt like that old joke about the writer who gets stranded on a desert island and ends up building two different publishing houses on opposite sides. *Why two?* someone asks, when he's finally rescued. *This, here, is the press where I send my work*, he responds, *and over there is the one where I'd never submit!*

And before we knew it, we couldn't even define what a prose poem was. All we knew was that everywhere we went, we felt like outsiders—we didn't fit in with the paragraphs, we didn't fit in with the poems, we didn't even fit in with each other.

Eventually, that seemed like the only thing that defined us— that ever-insistent sense of both belonging and not belonging, of being between and beyond genres.

What else could we do but try to seek something holy in that—to find hope in liminality, put our faith in ambiguity, believe in the great power of contradictions.

How Words Mean

I F *THE EAR is the only true writer*, as Frost writes, then I am in trouble because, for the past two weeks, I've barely been able to hear a thing. The muffling inside my head is so intense that, every time I sit down to write, it is as though all my antennas are broken, every radio station playing nothing but static. I pick up a pen, hoping to be lifted by the buoyancy of my ideas, and instead find only the roar of the ocean.

The otolaryngologist tells me that there is nothing to worry about, that I just have a little fluid trapped behind my eardrums: *No risk of permanent hearing loss*, she says. *No signs of systemic failure.*

She tears off a sheet from her pad and hands me a note with my official diagnosis: Clogged Sinuses.

There is something fascinating about seeing the word *sinuses* on paper—as though the word itself is some sort of concrete poem, its winding letters strung together to resemble the curvy cavity inside our heads.

It makes me think about all the work that goes into developing a font, how typefaces, as Sarah Hyndman writes, can *stimulate responses independently of the words they spell out.*

We spend so much time thinking about the semantic meaning of words when we write—carefully considering all the various tones—that it's easy to forget our emotional response often stems from the mere shape of the letters.

And maybe I've been spending a little too much time tapping out letters with my five-year-old as she learns to read, but there is something strangely satisfying about saying the word *clogged*, one phonetic unit at a time, something that I do over and over and over again on my drive home.

C-lo-gg-ed. C-lo-gg-ed. C-lo-gg-ed.

Unlike certain words whose sounds contravene their meanings, like *pulchritude*, which refers to *beauty* but sounds like the stomach flu, or *chlamydia*, which rolls off the tongue like the name of an Egyptian queen, the word *clogged* offers the perfect marriage of sound and sense, a monosyllabic word jam-packed with both hard consonants (*c- g- d-*) and the free-flowing *-lo-*.

And it is the interplay of those phonemes—the tension between the obstinate consonants bookending the word and the mellifluous notes in the middle—that almost embodies the physical sensation of having fluid trapped in one's ear.

This, of course, applies to some of the other words that we use to describe the same sensation, *plugged*, say, or *blocked*, but in these cases the *p-* is whispered and *b-* is barely voiced, and so we don't get the same effect of the hard crackling *c-* at the beginning of *clogged*.

It reminds me of what Ben Shahn means when he describes *form* as *the shape of content*.

Words, like poems, communicate in many ways, but more and more I find myself interested in understanding how both their shapes and sounds simultaneously reflect and affect their meanings.

This is why I almost half expected the doctor to tell me that my current medical predicament was not simply the result of a nasty cold but some sort of metaphysical condition—the physical manifestation of my *unique inscape*, as Hopkins termed it, as though all that white noise making it impossible to hear was the product of my soul's ever-insistent desire to tune out the external world and attend, instead, to the internal pressures inside my head.

The Marks We Leave Behind

M Y FIVE-YEAR-OLD loves to pee in the bathwater.

Even if I force her to sit on the toilet before she gets into the bath, she will squeeze her root chakras just before she's done peeing so that upon climbing into the tub, she can release the remains of whatever urine she'd secretly stashed in her bladder.

I tell her that this is gross. She tells me that she doesn't care.

I am convinced that there is something primal about this ritual—her way of marking her territory so that her sister doesn't try to take a bath with her. And yet despite its somewhat animalistic nature, I can't help but also see something literary in it.

Whenever I begin a new poem, one of the first things I do is list all of my most private and vulnerable thoughts related to the subject. In some ways, this is about marking my territory— filtering big ideas through a personal lens in order to help me locate a more distinct voice. But in other ways, like a five-year-old peeing in the bathwater, it's about forcing myself to sit in my own mess, making sure that I am writing from the perspective of my most imperfect and human self.

But it's one thing to mark your own territory, another to mark someone else's.

Last night I was at my desk, writing comments all over my students' stories when my five-year-old wandered on over, took a big old swig from my can of seltzer, rinsed vigorously, then slowly spat said swig back into the can before walking away with it.

That was mine, I said.

Not anymore, she said.

And although I was a little bitter and a lot disgusted, the more I thought about it the more I realized that I was essentially doing the same thing to my students' papers.

My students had entrusted me with their original stories and here I was vigorously marking them up with my red pen, contaminating their ideas with my own thoughts and suggestions. Surely tomorrow, when I returned their work to them, they would look at their marked-up stories and think, *That was mine*. And I would just walk away to the other side of the room and say, *Not anymore*.

I looked over at my five-year-old and told her that I wanted my seltzer back. She let out a loud unapologetic burp, then walked on over and placed the empty can on my desk.

And as I returned my attention to the stack of stories in front of me, I tried to remember that there was a difference between offering critical feedback and tainting my students' sense of ownership, that my job was not to mark up their stories but to help them make a mark of their own.

Poetry and Portals

I T's TWO in the morning when your five-year-old wakes you up and tells you that her belly is too full to sleep.

Try lying on your left side, you say. But she insists that she is going to be sick.

So, you walk her to the bathroom where the two of you just kind of hang out for a couple of minutes waiting for something to happen. *I think you're OK,* you say. But then she starts making this strange guttural noise in the back of her throat.

You rub her back as she bends over the toilet, and then, for some reason that you may never understand, just as her gurgles begin to morph into a heave, she pivots right and throws up all over your feet, a big old chunky stew of rice and carrots.

I feel better now, she says, then walks back to her room, climbs into her bed, and promptly falls back to sleep.

You clean up what you can, then go back to your own bed, but your mind is already spiraling up and down your to-do list. So you get up and make coffee and head to your desk to watch highlights from last night's game before opening your journal.

Against your better judgment, you begin describing the slimy bits of carrots still wedged between your toes. *It's the kind of itch you can't quite wash away,* you write. And then: *the kind of itch that approaches your sole.*

You regret this right away. Poetry is no place for dad puns.

And yet, you sense something metaphysical going on and wonder if there is an etymological link between *sole* and *soul*.

You consider researching this but don't, because you've never really trusted people who use the word *soul* in poems. Still, your mind is itching now, and you start thinking about the other meaning of *sole*—no, not the *flat fish*—but *sole* as in *lone*, as in the root of *solitude*.

You get up to refill your coffee cup, and when you come back, you see the phrase *root of solitude* and imagine a single tree in a barren landscape, its long-reaching roots humming underground. You realize that *sole* and *soil* are probably somehow related, and it suddenly strikes you as strange that the loneliest word in the English language could be connected to so many other words.

This feels like it has philosophical implications, and you wonder if being alone is the foundation of a rich spiritual life and what it would be like to live a more *solitary* existence—to have all that time to read and write and think.

Your mind is leaping now, not with connections per se, but associations, and you suddenly have this memory of playing *solitaire* with your grandfather when you were a kid—how he'd set out a deck for you and a deck for him, and the two of you would just sit there playing next to one another, alone and together at the same time.

You've only been writing for what feels like a few minutes now, but somehow the sun is starting to rise.

You write *sun = sol* in your journal, but that's more of a pothole than a portal at this point because you've already found your subject—the tension between the desire to be alone and the desire to feel deeply connected.

Though it's not solely the ideas that interest you now as much as the thrill of seeing all those meanings buzz beneath a single word.

What I've Learned about Literary Movements from My Daughters

M Y OLDER DAUGHTER has always been transfixed by the moon.

When she was a baby, we would sit on the back porch and watch it rise over our neighbor's house. She would clap her hands wildly and rub her chest. *Please*, she would beg me to climb into the night sky and retrieve it for her.

And although it's been seven years since those enchanting evenings, she still finds so much delight, say, in spotting a faded crescent among the morning clouds.

There is something about her relationship with the moon that reminds me of the great Romantic poets—the way she believes in our transcendent connection to nature, stares up at the sky with a never-ending sense of fascination.

My younger daughter, on the other hand, is obsessed with a different kind of moon—why wait for the waxing and waning of some faraway thing when you can walk into any room, drop your pants, and let the world know: *I got your moon right here.*

For while my older daughter might be a firm subscriber to the ideals of Romanticism, my younger daughter has aligned herself with the Modernists and their grand, sweeping rejection of decorum.

Not that she is necessarily trying to evoke the moral decay and wasteland of the Western world every time she hitches her thumbs into her waistband and launches into the old yank and bend.

Nor do I think that she's interested in reminding us of Freud's notion that we all long for more authentic ways to express our hidden selves.

Mostly, I think she just loves the power of being able to shift the mood in the room whenever she hears adults speaking in hushed tones, say, or whenever she senses something solemn in the air.

Literary movements come and go, and *isms* wax and wane, but watching my daughters reminds me that we must always make room for both reverence and irreverence in whatever we write, find ways to accept that life is simultaneously ridiculous and filled with so much splendor.

Why Write When There Are Thousands of People Out There Not Reading Your Work?

WE WERE at the home of some friends when I found myself in a conversation with their six-year-old son.

My dad told me that you're a writer, he said.

I am, I said.

Then let me ask you something, he said. *How come I've never read anything you wrote?*

That's a good question, I said.

Think about it, he said. *Right now there are thousands of people out there who aren't reading any of your books.*

He shook his head and walked away, leaving me all alone in the kitchen.

I grabbed a slice of lukewarm pizza and started laughing to myself. I'd recently published a small book of short prose and was well aware of all those people out there not reading it. It got me thinking about one of the two recurring dreams that I'd been having of late, which involved me walking into a bookstore to give a reading and seeing that there was only one person in the audience.

This, in fact, actually happened to me once, and although I laughed it off at the time—cracked some joke about the sound of one hand clapping—it was one of those moments that remind you of the fine line between *humility* and *humiliating*.

We left our friends' house shortly afterward, and although it was getting late, we decided to give our five-year-old a bath.

Giving our five-year-old a bath is always a bit of a production: she likes to bring trays of Tupperware into the tub with her and pretend that she's the star of some warped Disney film.

Look, I overheard her say at one point as I was walking by. *I know you think that you killed my parents. But I have news for you. It is I who poisoned your parents!*

Then she started laughing this evil, maniacal laugh.

I have no idea what the premise of her story was, but I wasn't about to ask, because if she knew that I was eavesdropping, she would have immediately stopped the show.

And as I stood in the hallway listening in, I started thinking about the other recurring dream that I'd been having as of late. In this one, I am taking a shower, and when I step out, I realize that there is a full crowd of people waiting for me to read. I walk up to the podium, and not only do I not have my book with me, I'm not wearing any pants.

I had always assumed that this was simply the converse of the first dream—rather than showing up with something to say and finding no one there, I show up with nothing to say and find everyone there.

But as I listened to my daughter play so freely in the bath—her imagination wandering in the most surprising and delightful of ways—I wondered if this dream was actually about the tension between the pleasures of writing and the pressures of being a writer.

On my better days, I'm able to compartmentalize the two. But whenever I've sat down to write lately, I've found myself worrying about book sales and Goodreads ratings, about the reviews that people were writing and the reviews that people weren't writing.

My five-year-old was starting to sing some song that could only be described as a ballad to her bum. I couldn't make out all the lyrics, though, because she was laughing so hard as she belted it out.

And I realized that if I wanted to reclaim the pleasures of writing, I couldn't worry about all those thousands of people not reading my books. Because that's not why we write. We write for *that single fleeting moment*, as Merce Cunningham says, *when [we] feel alive.*

The Creative Process in Four Easy Steps

M Y FIVE-YEAR-OLD has strep throat.

The good thing about strep throat is that, as soon as you start taking penicillin, you immediately feel better. The bad thing about strep throat is that penicillin is pink and goopy and smells like moldy chalk, and my daughter refuses to touch it.

It's a delicate situation, but luckily I happen to be taking an online course on *The Creative Process* and am well versed in the four easy steps of creative problem-solving!

Step One: Preparation

THE FIRST STEP of the creative process is *Preparation*, where you immerse yourself in a problem, then spend months researching, ideating, and tinkering. Creativity experts stress the importance of taking your time to fully understand the depths and complexity of the problem that you are trying to solve.

However, according to the very first article that I read on WebMD, it's actually dangerous to leave strep throat untreated for months, so instead of continuing to research, I just jump right in and tell my daughter that it's not a choice. She has to take her medicine.

This doesn't work, of course, but it's not *supposed* to work. The first idea is almost always the worst idea. If it worked, there would be no need to be creative!

The whole point of creativity is to come up with novel ideas, and one of the ways that we do this is through something called divergent thinking. Divergent thinking is the process of coming up with as many original and different ideas as you can. This can be really hard if you don't have ADHD. But one of the key things to remember when thinking divergently is that there are no wrong answers. You just have to let yourself go and come up with as many different ideas as possible!

And so, first, I explain to my five-year-old that she should be grateful that we live in a time period when medicine is readily available and people don't die of infected paper cuts.

That doesn't work. So, I dip into my understanding of extrinsic motivation and throw out a bunch of baseless bribes and idle threats.

That also doesn't work. But that's OK. As Edison said, *I didn't fail 1,000 times. The light bulb was an invention with 1,000 steps.*

So, I take out one of her teddy bears and create this elaborate play in which her teddy bear takes her medicine and loves it so much that she does this really hilarious happy dance, then gets to eat pretend jelly beans. Also doesn't work.

So instead, I try pinning my daughter down and plugging her nose so that she has to open her mouth to breathe, and then with my other hand, I use a plastic syringe to shoot the medicine down her throat.

This almost works, except my daughter pretends that she's a sperm whale and blows the whole thing out all over my glasses.

After I finish wiping my face with a towel, I make up a story about a kid I once knew who refused to take medicine and had to go to the doctor to get a really, really, really painful penicillin shot in the butt.

But my daughter is still at that age where she thinks that butts are the funniest thing in the world, and she just starts laughing and laughing and asks me to tell her that story again.

I find myself running out of ideas, and so, in a moment of desperation, I threaten to take her favorite blankie away for the rest of the summer if she doesn't take her medicine.

She glares at me and says, *If you do that, I will cut you open and rip out your stomach and all of your bones.*

Clearly, no one has explained to my five-year-old that in divergent thinking activities, you are supposed to defer judgment. Because once you start shooting down other people's ideas, they feel less free to ideate.

And now, we've reached a total standstill. It's like that old problem about an unstoppable force meeting an immovable object.

But that's OK—creativity is all about paradox!

And the reality is that, oftentimes when working creatively, you have to hit rock bottom. That's just part of the process. It's all about the process! You get yourself locked into some sort of really intricate problem where there's no way out, and then, guess what? You step away, and the solution just comes to you.

That's where Step Two comes in.

Step Two: Incubation

INCUBATION IS the stage of the creative process where you let ideas play around in your subconscious while you go for a long walk, and lo and behold, it's almost time to pick my older daughter up from camp, and her bus stop just happens to be a ten-minute walk away. So I ask my wife to take over with my five-year-old while I head off to incubate.

There is something about walking that immediately clears your mind and allows you to move into a space of deep contemplation, and by the time I reach the sidewalk, I realize that this battle has nothing to do with the taste of the medicine.

This is about control.

My five-year-old lives in a world where everyone is always telling her what to do. But mostly me. I'm the one that's always telling her what to do. And what I really need to do right now is manipulate her into thinking that she is the one making the decision to take her medicine all by herself. This is called empowerment.

As soon as I realize this, I am ready to move on to Step Three.

Step Three: Illumination

ILLUMINATION IS the instant when all those ideas in your subconscious that have been interplaying in dynamic ways finally merge together and you have your *Eureka!* moment.

I've read illumination typically happens after incubation, but for some reason, today steps two and three kind of happened simultaneously. And now that I think about it, the whole thing seems so obvious. How did I not figure this out three hours ago?

And now I'm not exactly sure what to do because I still have eight and a half minutes to go before I reach the bus stop, and I'm not really sure if you're allowed to incubate after you've already illuminated.

So, what I start doing is daydreaming (also very important to the creative process!) that I am some sort of wizard who knows how to play mind tricks on my five-year-old to get her to take her medicine. It is a really good daydream, and I get so into it that I almost walk past the bus stop where my seven-year-old is waiting for me.

By the time we get back home, I'm ready for Step Four.

Step Four: Verification

VERIFICATION IS the part of the process where you test out your ideas. You see, creative ideas not only have to be original; they also have to work! That's the beauty of it.

I rush in and tell my wife that all we need to do is convince my five-year-old that taking her medicine is a step toward her own self-actualization.

My wife gives me that smile, the one that makes me feel really smart, and then tells me that, as soon as I left, my daughter asked if she could just mix the medicine with chocolate ice cream, and then she slurped the whole thing down.

And now I'm not really sure what to do, because—how are you supposed to verify something that's already been verified? All I know is that it's really hard to master the creative process when my daughters keep undermining everything that I am learning.

I sit my five-year-old down and try explaining to her that according to all the articles that I've been reading and all of the TED Talks that I've been watching and all of the podcasts that I've been listening to, this isn't how the creative process is supposed to work.

But she just stares at me and smiles, a big old ring of chocolate ice cream covering her mouth, and I know that I wouldn't want it any other way.

The Long and Arduous Journey
of a Teeny-Weeny Word

I AM COOKING DINNER when my seven-year-old limps on over to me, struggling to catch her breath.

What's the matter? I ask.

We were wrestling, she says, *and I got kicked in the wienie.*

You don't have a wienie, I say.

Oh, she says.

And then, with a look of great concern, she asks, *What's a wienie?*

I usually try to outsource these kinds of questions to my wife. But my wife, ironically enough, is at the library photocopying materials for a Sex Ed course that she is preparing to teach.

And so, I put my wooden spoon down and try to explain to my seven-year-old that a *wienie* is, in fact, a *penis*.

My daughter stares at me blankly, and I am nervous about where this is going next, worried that one question will lead to another, and before I know it, I'll find myself in the middle of *the talk*.

But just as I brace for the worst, she opens her mouth and asks, *Why do people use the word* wienie *for* penis?

And I am suddenly overcome with gratitude that, of all the possible questions my daughter could have posed, she chose an etymological one.

For the word *wienie* has made a fascinating journey from the banks of the Danube to playgrounds all across America.

Like many food-related words, it initially referred to the place where it originated from, *Wien* being the German word for *Vienna*.

Unlike the macho sausages made in Frankfurt, which were associated with imperial coronations, the ones from *Wien* were softer and smaller in size and thus simply became known as *Wieners*.

And given that Freud himself was from Vienna, is it any surprise that these cased links were soon linked to the male anatomy? And thus, *wiener* became the slang term that kids still sling around today.

My daughter looks as though she is trying to slink away, but I'm not quite done because the word *wiener* is slightly different from the word *wienie*. And while one could make the case that Americans simply love informal nicknames, it's important to note that the word *wienie* is a homophone to the word *weeny*.

The word *weeny*—derived from a combination of the words *wee* and *tiny*—refers to a very small and adorable little thing. So, by shortening the word *wiener* to *wienie,* we are not just referring to the male anatomy but associating it with an itsy, bitsy, teeny-weeny one.

As I explain all of this to my daughter, it strikes me as rather remarkable that a word could have traveled so far to emasculate so many.

Perhaps equally remarkable is that my daughter is so bored at this point that she simply skips on back to the family room to continue roughhousing with her sister.

And as I return to tending the soup, it occurs to me that focusing on the historical evolution of words has the potential to get me out of almost any conversation that I don't want to have in the first place.

Though, later that evening, when my five-year-old and I are wrestling and she accidentally kicks me in the wienie and then asks with great concern, *Did I get you in the vagina?,* I am stumped, bewildered even, and realize that a firm understanding of etymology will only get my daughters so far in this life.

For everything else, they'll need their mother.

Why We Keep Journals

WE ARE STAYING at a family farm in New Hampshire, and I am sitting by the fire, journal in my lap, when you sit down beside me.

Why are you always writing in your journal? you ask.

I tell you that I am recording the small details of our trip to help me remember them later—descriptions, for example, of the four eggs that were still warm when I gathered them from the nest, how I had to use hay to wipe the poop off one before putting it in the carton.

You smile and rest your head on my arm.

What I don't tell you is that describing those eggs is my way of entertaining my latest minor existential crisis. Because while you and your younger sister were off doing arts and crafts—adding googly eyes to clothespins—I wandered over to the chicken coop and found a dead hen in the middle of the floor.

The other chickens had gathered around it and were pecking viciously at an open wound, which had turned raw and bloody. I stood there for a few moments, fascinated by the carnage, before I realized that I better alert a staff member before any kids wandered in.

But as I was about to leave, I noticed four perfect ovals in the nesting boxes in the back. And though it felt wrong to walk past the debauchery and take those eggs, I wanted so badly to show them to you—how each was a different size and color, how farm eggs have so much more personality than the ones you buy in a store.

And you and your sister were giddy when I showed you that one was too big to fit in the carton, that another was as blue as a robin's egg.

You went off to play after that, and I wandered to this rocking chair and started thinking about how, back when I was in college, I would head down to Chinatown to watch a shop owner slaughter chickens.

It wasn't the violence that repelled me back then but the awful sense of disconnect—how easily I could disassociate a dead animal from a deli sandwich. I visited that shop every few days, forcing myself to watch until I could no longer compartmentalize the two, until I chose to give up meat from any animal that I did not slaughter with my own two hands.

I wish that my turn to conscientious eating had felt like a moral victory, but the truth is—misguided as this now sounds—I was also angry and embarrassed that I hadn't come to this realization earlier in my life, as though it was one more reminder of my sheltered existence, one more instance of the world hiding its brutality from me.

And now I'm choosing to hide the brutality of the world from you, to let you be innocent and happy a little bit longer.

Though I know, too, that you are sitting beside me because there has been conflict all day between you and your friends—drama over who ditched whom to play with someone else—and now everyone's mad and hurt and wary of the pecking order.

Not that you'd ever admit this to me. It's so much easier to pretend like everything's OK.

And so, I offer you a sheet from my journal—a page from my book—and you begin writing your own private thoughts, each of us lost in our own silent truths as the fire burns in front of us, its chaotic flames contained in the hearth.

On the Many Meanings of *Seal*:
An Origin Story

IN COLLEGE, I was much more sensitive than most of my friends, but I'd learned to disguise the difference with a mask of indifference, convinced that real men were supposed to be emotionally sealed off from the world. And then a childhood friend of mine collapsed and died of a heart attack in the middle of a lacrosse game, and when I sat down to fill out a card for his sister, everything just poured out of me. I wrote so much that I had to buy another card and then another and then another, and although I never sent any of them, I still recall that feeling of looking at a blank card and seeing a fresh new page.

A few weeks later, I bought my first book of poems and remember wondering if I was supposed to read them in order or if I was allowed to flip around. I had only ever read poems in school, where we were forced to mark each one up and encouraged to think of literary analysis as a form of combat, as though we were Navy SEALs on a stealthy mission to wrestle each poem to the ground, to attack them with our pens, to dismantle them in order to extract their meanings.

★

Later that spring, I signed up for a poetry class with a professor who seemed to confuse *author* with *authority*. He was a lawyer before turning to poetry and spoke with the fervor of the recently converted, held strong opinions about anapests and dactyls, and spent the first month of the class focused entirely on prosody. He had a riveting mind, but there was little room for creative expression in our own work, and when we wrote, we did so hoping for his seal of approval.

Then, one night, some friends and I went to a reading of a poet who'd recently won a number of prizes for his latest collection. I'd desperately wanted to understand his poems, but the truth was that I struggled to follow any of them on even the most syntactical of levels. *When I was younger*, he said at one point between poems, *I did a lot of acid, and one evening, I wandered on over to the bay and came upon a pod of barking seals, and in my hallucinatory state, I joined them, barking at the moon alongside them until I felt like I, too, was a seal. Writing poetry is my way of slipping on the skin of my seal self, of returning to the wildness and wilderness of that night.*

I went back to my dorm after that convinced that I would never be a poet—I had never dropped acid, never barked with marine mammals in the bay. At best, I was interested in playing with words until they revealed, as Frost writes, *something I didn't know I knew*. Part of the problem, I think, is that I held onto this romantic notion that one didn't learn to write poetry. One was born a poet. It was a matter of destiny, and my fate, unfortunately, was sealed.

I took some time off the following year to travel abroad, where I fell violently ill with dysentery and a bacterial infection that left me temporarily deaf on my left side. One night, as I was shivering on my cot in a youth hostel, pus began to ooze out of my ear. Convinced that something in my brain had burst, I wrote my parents a feverish ten-page letter, then sealed it shut, wrapped myself tightly in a blanket, and sank into the depths of my soul before I died.

★

I survived, of course, and threw that letter away the next morning, embarrassed to have mistaken an ear infection for a brain aneurysm. And yet, something else inside me had burst open. It would still be years before I would read Lorca's writings on *duende,* but I was convinced by now that poetry would help me find a path back to that deep, deep sense of self. The world was filled with magic and suffering. I had so much to say and no one to say it to. My heart was opened, but my lips were sealed.

Lambie, Lambie, Burning Bright

I asked my eight-year-old what would be the first thing that she would buy if she had her own money. *I'm not sure*, she said, *but it definitely wouldn't be anything made out of plastic because that's bad for the earth, and I think I'd want something that would keep me healthy.*

It was such a virtuous response that it reminded me of why the Romantic poets always associated childhood with purity and thought of youth as *Nature's priests*—a sentiment that is perhaps best shown in William Blake's illustrated poem, "The Lamb."

The Lamb

> Little Lamb who made thee
>   Dost thou know who made thee
> Gave thee life & bid thee feed.
> By the stream & o'er the mead;
> Gave thee clothing of delight,
> Softest clothing wooly bright;
> Gave thee such a tender voice,
> Making all the vales rejoice!
>   Little Lamb who made thee
>   Dost thou know who made thee
>
>   Little Lamb I'll tell thee,
>   Little Lamb I'll tell thee!
> He is called by thy name,
> For he calls himself a Lamb:
> He is meek & he is mild,

He became a little child:
I a child & thou a lamb,
We are called by his name.
    Little Lamb God bless thee.
    Little Lamb God bless thee.

It makes sense why Blake would include this in a collection called *Songs of Innocence*, given that it is filled with words such as *lamb, life, delight, bright, tender, rejoice,* and *bless*—but I'm more interested here in looking at how Blake handles the content of the poem, reinforcing its theme of innocence through its remarkably balanced composition.

One way that poets create a sense of order is through music, and Blake offers us an even and regular meter running throughout every line. The poem consists of two equal-sized stanzas—each made up of five rhyming couplets—and within each stanza, the beginning lines repeat at the end, offering us a sense of closure. The feeling of completion is further reinforced by another structural element: the first stanza poses questions, and the second answers them.

It reminds me of when my daughters were babies and filled with so much heartbreaking wonder and innocence, and how our love for them felt so uncomplicated and complete.

But we can't read "The Lamb," of course, without also reading "The Tyger," a poem that was published as its counterpoint five years later in Blake's *Songs of Experience*.

The Tyger

Tyger Tyger, burning bright,
In the forests of the night;
What immortal hand or eye,
Could frame thy fearful symmetry?

In what distant deeps or skies.
Burnt the fire of thine eyes?
On what wings dare he aspire?
What the hand, dare seize the fire?

And what shoulder, & what art,
Could twist the sinews of thy heart?
And when thy heart began to beat,
What dread hand? & what dread feet?

What the hammer? what the chain,
In what furnace was thy brain?
What the anvil? what dread grasp,
Dare its deadly terrors clasp!

When the stars threw down their spears
And water'd heaven with their tears:
Did he smile his work to see?
Did he who made the Lamb make thee?

Tyger Tyger burning bright,
In the forests of the night:
What immortal hand or eye,
Dare frame thy fearful symmetry?

The content of this poem is much more troubling than that of "The Lamb"—offering us such words as *burning, fearful, fire, dread, chain, deadly,* and *terrors*—but I'm again interested here in the handling of the content, and it's important to note that the composition of this poem is also quite orderly. We again have a regular meter running throughout every line. The poem consists of six equal-sized stanzas—each made up of rhyming couplets—and as in "The Lamb," Blake uses repeated lines at the beginning and conclusion of the poem.

But the best poems offer us *a genuinely threatening sense of disorder and an equally convincing order,* writes Gregory Orr.

The two forces together seek some balance, reconciliation, or resolution. And unlike "The Lamb," this poem does not offer us the structural balance of call and response. Instead, like an impatient child, it poses questions, then more questions, then more questions, then more questions, until it spirals into great existential doubt and asks: *Did he who made the lamb make thee?* And it is this combination of order and chaos that makes "The Tyger" so compelling. There is symmetry, but it is a fearful symmetry—like the appearance of twins in a horror film.

However, while it is Blake's unanswered questions that unsettle us with great uncertainty, sometimes the answers to questions can be equally disturbing. As when I turned to my six-year-old and asked her the same question that I had posed to my older daughter: *What would be the first thing you would buy if you had your own money?*

A tiger, she said without hesitating. *A tiger that kills people.*

And it wasn't just the content of her response that troubled me. It was the way that she said it in such a sweet angelic voice without any acknowledgement of irony or mischief, as she cuddled with her "Lovey" on the couch—a little white lamb that now looked troublingly limp in her arms.

Unhinged

W**E ARE WALKING** home from the farmers market when I pose the following riddle to my daughters:

> Mia and Maria are biological sisters who were born on the exact same day of the exact same year, and yet they are not twins. How is this possible?

Do they have the same dad but different moms? my eight-year-old asks.

Great question, I say. *But no.*

Do they have the same mom but different dads? my six-year-old asks.

I take a minute to think about how to best respond to this question before simply saying that, no, they both have the same mother and same father.

Did one travel from the past? From the future? Did they come from outer space?

There was nothing unusual about them, I say. *They were just regular sisters like the two of you.*

Were Mia and Maria dogs? my wife asks.

No, I say, *they were humans.*

It is quiet for a moment as we wait for some cars to pass by, and then my eight-year-old suddenly blurts out, *Are they part of a triplet?*

There must have been something about that image of a mama dog nursing a whole litter of puppies that triggered a connection in my daughter's mind, freed her to think outside the confines of the problem, and make the kind of associative leap that is essential to the creative process.

Later that afternoon, we are attending a neighbor's housewarming party, and I am upstairs on a self-guided tour of their recent renovations when I notice that all the bedroom doors have three hinges. This strikes me as strange because all the doors in our condo only have two hinges.

I kneel down, put my hands beneath the bottom of one of the doors, and lift ever so slightly, then start searching my pockets for a pen because I suddenly realize what's wrong with the poem I'd been working on since the morning.

I had been trying to forge a connection between two very different ideas with the equivalent of two hinges. And it was working but only because the ideas—like the doors in my condo—were hollow. I needed something with a little more heft, something so weighty that it would require a third hinge.

I start brainstorming how I might add more substance to the poem when it occurs to me that the *triplets* riddle might have somehow primed my imagination to make this connection.

I can feel myself starting to get super meta when two men walk out of the bathroom together. They are talking about the difficulty of laying tile and the challenge of getting rid of visible seams. One of them suggests tucking the edge of the wall tile under the ledge tile, and before I can even consider the metaphorical possibilities of that image, I suddenly feel so embarrassed that, here I am walking through this beautifully remodeled house, and instead of stealing home improvement ideas, I am thinking about poetry.

We've lived in our condo through eight sweltering summers, and I still haven't installed a single AC unit into any of the window frames. There is mildew in the bathroom, along with stripped screws in the stairwell and holes in the drywall that I haven't patched up because *spackle* is more fun to say than to use.

In place of a man cave, I have a poetry attic. You can't invite your boys over to watch football in a poetry attic.

It's as though I don't live in the physical world. Even now, I'm not just in a hallway—I am lost in some existential limbo, considering the metaphysical nature of hinges when I should be figuring out how to provide a better home, no, house, for my family.

I head back downstairs, and even that feels metaphorical—a descent into the depths of my own self-pity—when I see my wife sitting at the most beautiful kitchen island I have ever seen.

She has this radiant smile on her face, and I am convinced that she, too, is lost in thought, probably fantasizing about Bob Vila, a returned Peace Corps volunteer actually worth marrying.

I walk on over to her and am prepared to apologize for the failed state of our marriage when she lowers her eyes and whispers, *Have you tried the brie?*

I glance over at the counter beside us, and there it is—a whole wheel of baked brie covered in caramel and pecans—and I realize that my wife is not thinking about how much more beautiful this home is than ours because she is lost in a sweet and creamy wheel of sensory delight.

I have never been so grateful for soft cheese in all my life.

I grab a plate, and the two of us stand there, indulging. All around us, people are commenting on backsplashes and sight lines, and although I know that I probably should be taking mental notes on whether I am resting my elbows on quartz or granite, I don't care.

I feel so lucky to be attached to this woman who is clearly meant for me, who doesn't mind that I think more about counterpoints than countertops, and I am overcome with gratitude to have this moment together—just the two of us—as though this luxurious kitchen island is an exotic island of our own.

A Sign of the Times

YOU NEVER FORGET your very first swastika.

I didn't see mine until I was nineteen years old, wandering the alleyways of Kathmandu with a Tibetan friend. We'd been discussing the similarities between Judaism and Buddhism when we ran into it—a giant swastika spray-painted on a wall. I stopped and stared, desperately trying to figure out how to register what I was seeing.

It's one of our most auspicious signs, my friend told me. *It signifies prosperity.*

What do you mean by prosperity? I said.

Good luck, he said. *Like these*, pointing to the rabbits on the back of his shoes.

Under different circumstances, I might have told my friend that the auspicious rabbits on the heels of his sneakers were actually *Playboy* bunnies, but I couldn't stop staring at the swastika, paralyzed by the strange and sobering emotions that it was triggering inside of me.

I lost most of my family during the Holocaust, but the only swastikas I'd ever personally encountered were in history books or museums. Despite having grown up as one of only a few Jews in a small, sleepy town on the coast of Maine, I had never felt threatened, only out of place. At worst, teachers would schedule quizzes on Rosh Hashanah every year, and shop clerks reminded you of your otherness with their relentless Christmas cheer.

So, there was something both eerie and absurd about seeing this giant swastika—which was oddly upright and painted counterclockwise—out in the open for everyone to see, as though it were just some big, harmless geometric figure. It almost looked like two graceful dancers in the middle of the tango or a crossword puzzle that you might attempt over a latte on a lazy Sunday—so different from the two small swastikas that I came across this morning at the playground down the street from my house.

My older daughter had been rollerblading with my wife on the basketball court while I was busy chasing my younger daughter around the playground when I found the swastikas etched into a slide with a knife. My six-year-old flew right past them and waited for me at the bottom, but I paused where I was, again, struggling to register what I was seeing.

I imagine that if we had encountered these in a different town, it would have simply felt disconcerting, a sign of the political times—but this was the playground that I had been taking my kids to since they were babies, in a progressive town with a sizable Jewish community.

I had no intentions of pointing them out to my kids, but when my older daughter overheard me speaking to my wife in hushed tones, she became alarmed and kept asking what we were talking about, and I knew that if I didn't show them to her, her imagination would lead her to far worse places.

I've often thought about how and when I would tell my daughters about the Holocaust. I've read about ways to approach such conversations so that they feel sensitive but honest, clear but brief. But it was always such a deeply personal and secretive story in my household when I was growing up that I struggled to imagine how I would ever enter that conversation.

My daughters had such unadulterated pride in being Jewish, such faith in the goodness of this world, and now, as my eight-year-old and I climbed the stairs to the slide, I worried that things were about to come crashing down.

What do they mean, she asked, when I pointed them out to her.

They're just a symbol, I said, *that some people write to make other people feel bad.*

Like for their religion? she asked.

I don't know how she knew, but she knew.

Yeah, I said, *like for their religion.*

She looked at them, then up at me, then said OK and slid down the slide so she could run back to the basketball court to draw with chalk.

And although I knew that neo-Nazis were not taking over my neighborhood, that white supremacists were not hanging out on the local playgrounds, that this was probably etched by some twelve-year-old without any understanding of its history or impact, it still felt so deeply unsettling to see these tiny swastikas and how they looked just like the ones you see in old books—like swirling tornadoes or a tangling of limbs, one body tumbling forward while the other stumbles backward, a tilting of history and the off-kilter intersection of fates.

Same Place, Same Time

THE ADVANTAGE to signing both daughters up for the same dance class was that for one hour every Sunday, they were contractually obligated to be in the same place at the same time. The disadvantage was that, while the class offered my older daughter a chance to shine, my younger daughter constantly found herself on the wrong side of Vygotsky's *zone of proximal development*.

This was tolerable in a self-contained studio, but as soon as they began preparing for the end-of-year recital, my younger daughter started growing more and more anxious and resistant by the day. And on the evening of their dress rehearsal, when their instructor announced that it was time for all dancers in the auditorium to participate in the opening number, my eight-year-old sprinted up onto the stage while my six-year-old pivoted and bolted straight into my arms.

I'm not ready, she sobbed, her head buried into my chest.

The music started blaring, and my older daughter started twirling, waving her arms from side to side and clapping her hands in a Z formation. She was glowing—as confident as I had ever seen her—but I couldn't quite figure out how to cheer for her while simultaneously comforting her sister.

I tried alternating my selective attention, which worked OK at first, though soon enough, I was whispering, *You're doing great*, to my six-year-old and cheering, *It's gonna be OK!* to my eight-year-old.

The ensemble ended, and all the dancers returned to their seats so that each troupe could perform their individual dances. I somehow pried my six-year-old off my neck and convinced her to sit on her sister's lap, and she seemed to regain her composure enough to enjoy the other numbers.

Then it was time for them to perform, and their teacher led them onto the stage. My eight-year-old struck a glamorous pose in the front row while my six-year-old stood behind her, knees shaking and chest heaving. And I couldn't figure out which daughter to focus on.

Poetry, of course, thrives on mixed emotions, on the ability to hold contradictory ideas in one's head and opposing feelings in one's heart. *I am large, I contain multitudes*, Whitman famously writes, and that desire to make sense of duality is what keeps us writing throughout the years.

But I wasn't prepared for this sudden ambush of private emotions in such a public space, my heart swirling with terror and pride, as though it, too, was being forced to dance—split jumping and half breaking to the music.

My six-year-old was shaking so hard, she looked like she was doing jazz hands with her entire body. I wanted to rescue her. I wanted to run up on stage and scoop her into my arms and protect her from every miserable character-building moment of childhood.

And then something turned.

It was as though my younger daughter suddenly forgot about all the people in the auditorium, and with a single pirouette, she let go of all her fear and started waving her arms in the air.

Something gave inside of me, as though there was no greater story in this world than the one in which we overcome our fears and realize that we are stronger than we thought we were. And although I knew that the world would upend this narrative again and again, that courage was tentative and self-realization elusive, I didn't care. I watched my daughters up on that stage, and for the briefest of moments, I could feel all our hearts moving to this joyous beat in unison.

Why Teaching Creative Writing
Is Essential

S HORTLY AFTER the pandemic started, my family and I were listening to the news when we heard that Florida had designated pro wrestling as an essential business. My six-year-old pumped her fists in the air, thrilled to see her love of roughhousing finally validated. But my eight-year-old looked troubled.

Why would anyone consider wrestling to be existential? she asked.

My daughter had meant to say *essential,* of course (and how she knows the word *existential* in the first place involves a long story about a joke that I used to make her tell when she was three about an existential cough named *cough-ka*). But since I'm an English teacher who's currently struggling to figure out how to engage students through remote learning, it got me thinking about the link between *essential* and *existential.*

I teach creative writing classes at a public high school outside of Boston. I'm not sure if anyone has ever considered creative writing to be essential, but it's certainly existential. *What are your characters' underlying motivations?* my students regularly ask each other. *What are their biggest doubts?*

But teaching creative writing remotely has been challenging. I miss the energy and chaos of the classroom. I miss the messiness of guiding kids through the creative process. Like many schools, we've shifted to a pass/fail model. It's hard to motivate students to take the time to put *the best words in the best order* when, in the words of a colleague, *a D- is now worth the same as an A-.*

And yet my students continue to inspire me. Last week, I asked one class to write a short story in an alternative form—a police report, for example, or email exchange—and one of my seniors turned in a piece told entirely through Minecraft dialogue.

In the piece, the characters go by their screen names: Dufus, Lemonsquares, Potatosackpoopy. They are all teenage boys, trying to navigate the isolating challenges of quarantine by playing video games together, which offers them a chance to connect but also reveals some stunning disconnects. At one point, a character named Yomama420 suffers multiple deaths in the game:

> yomama420 was eaten by a zombie
> yomama420 was struck by lightning
> yomama420 was trampled to death by frightened shoppers
>   struggling for the last roll of charmin

And then, we see his friends' reactions:

> <clampgod9> LMAO didn't know that last one could happen
> <jayzseancarterbeyonce4ever> dire times call for dire measures haha
> <yomama420> actually guys gotta head to store for tp. mom's
>   struggling currently lol

In my student's reflection on the story, he wrote:

> I really like to look at the coronavirus numbers, be it the
> Johns Hopkins database or worldometer.com, and I think
> that's because it's innately satisfying for people to attempt
> to represent such an emotional tragedy that's unimaginable
> in scale numerically and with graphs, which . . . is much
> easier to digest. It removes names and to some extent the

weight of each individual death, softening the blow of each of the 200,000 deaths for my consumption. The way *Minecraft* conveys death seems similar to me.

I wanted to both laugh and cry when I read this, stunned by how my student had channeled the surreal disjunction that we have all been feeling into art.

Too often, under normal conditions, high school can feel like a game. Despite all the research showing that extrinsic motivation kills creativity, we rely systematically on extrinsic motivators. More often than not, students don't think of grades as an essential aspect of feedback but as a currency to trade in for college acceptances. We spend way too much time preparing kids for tests that don't assess meaningful skills but measurable ones.

However, as much as teaching during the pandemic has been challenging, I do think that it has reminded me to prioritize relationships. I have always been lucky to have supervisors who've stressed "relationship before task," but the pandemic has intensified the importance of this sentiment. I begin every email to my students with the reminder that their health is the most important thing right now. They end their emails to me: *I hope you and your family are safe*.

When we do return to the classroom, I hope that we continue to relate to one another with such humanity and care. That, of course, begins with me. I need to remember to ask myself every time I create an assignment: Will my students be intrinsically motivated to work on this? Will it offer them the chance to explore the world in profound ways?

I sometimes worry that the more existential a subject is, the less essential it is considered. But I want my students to know that wrestling—with language and ideas, with purpose and meaning—is the most essential thing of all.

Explaining to My Daughters Why I Wake Up at Three Every Morning to Write

THERE ARE the practical reasons, of course: if I want to write for a few hours a day while teaching full time and still being fully present for the two of you, I have to sacrifice something. I'm willing to sacrifice sleep.

And although there are days when it hurts to wake up, when the late afternoon headaches arrive by midmorning, for the most part, my body has been a willing coconspirator, a partner to the ambitions of my soul.

But to be honest, I've always been an early riser. Even at your age, I would wake up by dawn every morning to watch *Batman* with my older brothers. In college, it was to finish the papers I was supposed to have written the night before. In the Peace Corps, it was so I could run those dusty hills before the sun made it impossible to do just about anything.

Whatever its roots, I've always loved being awake before anyone else, grasping onto whatever solitude I can find.

There is something entrancing about writing before I am fully awake—my mind slipping back and forth between thoughts and dreams, my fingers trying to capture the images dancing in my head. I can't write poems in the afternoon. My mind is too fully conscious by then, too saddled by the details of the day, too anxious to get things done.

Once, when I was in college, I walked past an alleyway where someone had written in colorful graffiti: *Is it tomorrow or the end of the day?*

I loved the ambiguity of that question and all its existential implications. And now that I work in those intermediate hours, I can't help but think that this is what has led me to write so often about borderlands and liminalities, beginnings and ends.

I could probably answer your question about my writing habits a thousand times in a thousand different ways. Though I've learned, too, that sometimes a routine develops into a ritual and you just can't explain why.

Maybe you could take a day off every now and again, your mom will remind me when I look worn out before we even sit down to breakfast. But on those days when I don't write, I get stuck in false and petty narratives. Little things bother me. I judge myself relentlessly.

And I know, too, that when you asked me why I always get up so early, your question had a sting to it. You were really asking why I was not there for you when you woke up from a nightmare, when you needed me to rub your back so that you could fall back asleep—how you hated climbing the stairs to the cold and dark attic to call me down.

But the truth is this: just over eight years ago, at just past three in the morning, I transformed from a man into a father. And everything I ever thought I knew about life changed.

Now I head to my desk every morning and try to remember the miracle of being awake, try to return to that moment when I first held one of you in my arms.

The intellect of man is forced to choose, writes Yeats, *Perfection of the life, or of the work.*

It's never been a choice for me. Everything I write is a love letter to the two of you.

Works Referenced

"Allen Iverson's Legendary Practice Rant [FULL] | ESPN Archives." *YouTube*. Uploaded by ESPN, 7 May 2019. www.youtube.com/watch?v=K9ZQhyOZCNE.

Allen, William. *Conversations with Kurt Vonnegut*. Literary Conversations Series. University Press of Mississippi, 1988.

Amabile, Teresa, and Steven Kramer. *The Progress Principle: Using Small Wins to Ignite Joy, Engagement, and Creativity at Work*. Harvard Business Review Press, 2011.

Ammons, A. R. *Set in Motion: Essays, Interviews, and Dialogues*. Edited by Zofia Burr. University of Michigan Press, 2014.

Aristotle. *Poetics*. Edited by Malcolm Heath. Penguin Classics, 1996.

Aristotle, quoted in Adams Media, *Words of Art: Inspiring Quotes from the Masters*. Adams Media, 2013.

Auden, W. H. *Collected Poems*. Reprint, Vintage, 1991.

Baum, Devorah. *The Jewish Joke: An Essay with Examples: Less Essay, More Examples*. Profile Books, 2017.

Beckett, Samuel. *Worstward Ho*. Grove Press, 1983.

Berman, Ben. *Then Again*. Vine Leaves Press, 2018.

Berman, Noa and Sadie. Daughters. Quoted frequently and without permission.

Bishop, Elizabeth. "The Fish." In *Poems*. Farrar, Straus and Giroux, 2011.

Blake, William. *Songs of Innocence and Experience*. Penguin Pocket Poets (Penguin Clothbound Poetry). Penguin Classics, 2018.

Bly, Robert. *Iron John: A Book about Men*. 3rd ed. Da Capo Press, 2015.

Bradbury, Ray. *Zen in the Art of Writing: Essays on Creativity*. Joshua Odell Editions, 1994.

Campbell, Joseph. *The Hero's Journey: Joseph Campbell on His Life and Work*. Edited by Phil Cousineau. New World Library, 2014.

Carroll, Lewis. *Alice's Adventures in Wonderland & Through the Looking-Glass*. Bantam Classics, 1984.

"The Catcher in the Rye: Study Guide." *SparkNotes*. www.sparknotes.com/lit/catcher. Accessed 10 May 2019.

Cézanne, Paul, quoted in Bill Swainson, *Encarta Book of Quotations*. St. Martin's Press, 2000.

Coleridge, Samuel Taylor. *The Complete Poems*. Edited by William Keach. Penguin Classics, 2004.

Coleridge, Samuel Taylor, quoted in John Worthen, *The Cambridge Introduction to Samuel Taylor Coleridge*. Cambridge Introductions to Literature. Cambridge University Press, 2010.

Collins, Thomas, and Vivienne Rundle. *The Broadview Anthology of Victorian Poetry and Poetic Theory: Concise Edition*. Broadview Press, 2000.

Cooper, Robbie, et al. *Alter Ego: Avatars and Their Creators*. Chris Boot, 2009.

Croll, Morris W. "The Baroque Style in Prose." In *Style, Rhetoric, and Rhythm: Essays by Morris W. Croll*. Princeton University Press, 1966.

Csikszentmihalyi, Mihaly. *Creativity: Flow and the Psychology of Discovery and Invention*. HarperCollins, 1996.

Csikszentmihalyi, Mihaly. *Finding Flow: The Psychology of Engagement with Everyday Life*. Masterminds Series. Basic Books, 1998.

Daugherty, Tracy. *Let Us Build Us a City*. Crux: The Georgia Series in Literary Nonfiction. University of Georgia Press, 2017.

Derrida, Jacques. *Memoires for Paul de Man*. Revised edition. Columbia University Press, 1989.

Dove, Rita, quoted in David Drake, *Each of Us Is a Book: Poems for the Library Minded*. McFarland & Company, 2003.

Dunn, Stephen. *Walking Light*. Expanded ed. BOA Editions Ltd., 2001.

Eliot, Thomas Stearns. *Selected Prose of T. S. Eliot*. Edited by Frank Kermode. Harvest Books, 1975.

Éluard, Paul. *Œuvres complètes (Complete in Two Volumes)*. Edited by Lucien Scheler and Marcelle Dumas. Gallimard / Pléiade, 1968.

Fennelly, Beth Ann. "Reduced Sentences." *American Poetry Review*. aprweb.org/poems/reduced-sentences. Accessed 27 May 2018.

Fennelly, Beth Ann. *Heating & Cooling: 52 Micro-Memoirs*. W. W. Norton & Company, 2018.

Fitzgerald, F. Scott. *The Great Gatsby*. Scribner, 1925. Reprint, Scribner, 2004.

Foer, Jonathan Safran. *Here I Am*. Farrar, Straus and Giroux, 2016. Reprint, Picador Paper, 2017.

Foster, Thomas. *How to Read Literature Like a Professor*. Perfection Learning, 2014.

Frost, Robert. *The Collected Prose of Robert Frost*. Edited by Mark Richardson. Annotated edition. Belknap Press: An Imprint of Harvard University Press, 2010.

Frost, Robert. *The Letters of Robert Frost, Volume 1: 1886–1920*. Edited by Donald Sheehy, Mark Richardson, and Robert Faggen. Annotated edition. Belknap Press: An Imprint of Harvard University Press, 2014.

Frost, Robert. *The Poetry of Robert Frost: The Collected Poems*. Edited by Edward Connery Lathem. Henry Holt, 1969.

Gay, Ross. *The Book of Delights: Essays*. Algonquin Books, 2019.

Gay, Roxane. "Living with My Parents in Florida, It's Difficult to Feel like an Adult." *The Guardian*, 27 January 2015. www.theguardian.com/commentisfree/2015/jan/27/living-with-my-parents-in-florida-its-difficult-to-feel-like-an-adult.

Geisel, Theodor Seuss. *The Cat in the Hat*. Random House, 2013.

Georges, Danielle Legros. Interview by Jaime Kaiser. *The Editorial* 88 (9 Jan. 2017). https://www.theeditorial.com/essay/2016/9/6/danielle-legros-georges.

Greenberg, Irving. *Sage Advice: Pirkei Avot*. Maggid Books, 2016.

Hall, Donald. *Claims for Poetry*. Poets on Poetry. University of Michigan Press, 1982.

Harjo, Joy. *How We Became Human: New and Selected Poems 1975–2001*. W. W. Norton & Company, 2004.

Hayes, Terrance. *How to Be Drawn*. Penguin Poets. Penguin Books, 2015.

Hemingway, Ernest. Interview by George Plimpton. "The Art of Fiction No. 21." *The Paris Review* 18 (spring 1958). www.theparisreview.org/interviews/4825/the-art-of-fiction-no-21-ernest-hemingway.

Hirsch, Edward. *The Essential Poet's Glossary*. Mariner Books, 2017.

Hugo, Richard. *The Triggering Town: Lectures and Essays on Poetry and Writing*. Reissue edition. W. W. Norton & Company, 2010.

Hyndman, Sarah. *Why Fonts Matter*. Gingko Press, 2016.

James, Henry. "The Art of Fiction." *Longman's Magazine* 4 (September 1884).

James, William. *The Principles of Psychology*. Vol. 1. Henry Holt, 1893.

Jarrell, Randall. *Poetry and the Age*. University Press of Florida, 2001.

Kafka, Franz. *Letters to Friends, Family and Editors*. Edited by Richard Winston and Clara Winston. Schocken, 1990.

Kafka, Franz, quoted in M. P. Singh, *Quote, Unquote: A Handbook of Famous Quotations*. Lotus Press, 2006.

Keats, John. *Selected Letters*. Oxford World's Classics. Edited by Robert Gittings. With an introduction by Jon Mee. Critical ed. Oxford University Press, 2009.

Kelly, Richard, dir. *Donnie Darko*. Newmarket Films, 2001.

Kershner, Irvin, dir. *The Empire Strikes Back*. Twentieth Century-Fox Film Corporation, 1980.

Kingston, Maxine Hong. *I Love a Broad Margin to My Life*. Vintage International. Knopf, 2011. Reprint, Vintage, 2012.

Konnikova, Maria. *Mastermind: How to Think Like Sherlock Holmes*. Penguin Books, 2013.

Lawrence, D. H. *Selected Poems*. Penguin Classics, 2010.

Lehman, David. "Archie: A Profile of A. R. Ammons." Academy of American Poets. poets.org/text/archieprofile-r-ammons. Accessed 27 February 2019.

Levertov, Denise. *New and Selected Essays*. New Directions, 1992.

Lewis, C. S., quoted in Sy Safransky, *Sunbeams: A Book of Quotations*. Sun Publishing Company, 2012.

Lorca, Federico García. *Theory and Play of the Duende*. Kanathos, 1981.

Lynch, David. *Catching the Big Fish: Meditation, Consciousness, and Creativity*. 10th Anniversary Edition. TarcherPerigee, 2016.

Miłosz, Czeslaw. *The Collected Poems, 1931–1987*. The Ecco Press, 1988.

Moyers, Bill, quoted in Maria Popova, "What Is Creativity? Cultural Icons on What Ideation Is and How It Works." *The Marginalian*, 18 Sept. 2015. www.themarginalian.org/2013/09/06/what-is-creativity.

Orr, Gregory. *Richer Entanglements: Essays and Notes on Poetry and Poems*. Poets on Poetry. University of Michigan Press, 1994.

Orwell, George. *Why I Write: George Orwell Essays Book*. Sahara Publisher Books, 1946.

Osborne, Mark, and John Stevenson, dirs. *Kung Fu Panda*. Paramount Pictures, 2008.

Paley, Grace, quoted in Tracy Daugherty, *Let Us Build Us a City*. Crux: The Georgia Series in Literary Nonfiction. University of Georgia Press, 2017.

Picasso, Pablo, quoted in "Modern Living: Ozmosis in Central Park." *Time*, 4 October 1976.

Roethke, Theodore. *Straw for the Fire*. With an introduction by David Wagoner. Doubleday Anchor, 1974.

Ryan, Kay. Interview by Jessie Carty. "Cooling the Surface, Tending the Cracks: An Interview with Kay Ryan." *Drunken Boat* 11. d7.drunkenboat.com/db11/04kay/kay/interview.php.

Ryan, Kay. *Synthesizing Gravity: Selected Prose*. Grove Press, 2021.

Saunders, George. Interview by Stuart Hammond. "The Short Story Master Talks Drugs, Poverty, and the American Future . . ." *Dazed*, 31 December 2012. www.dazeddigital.com/artsandculture/article/15311/1/george-saunders.

Shahn, Ben. *The Shape of Content*. Charles Eliot Norton Lectures 1956–1957. 9th ed. Harvard University Press, 1985.

Shaiman, Mark, composer. *Hairspray: Soundtrack to the Motion Picture*. Watertower Music, 2007, compact disc.

Shankman, Adam, dir. *Hairspray*. New Line Cinema, 2007.

Shapiro, Alan. *That Self-Forgetful Perfectly Useless Concentration*. University of Chicago Press, 2016.

Shelley, Percy Bysshe, and Mary Wollstonecraft Shelley. *Essays, Letters from Abroad, Translations and Fragments*. William Smith, 1845.

Simic, Charles. *The Uncertain Certainty: Interviews, Essays, and Notes on Poetry*. Poets on Poetry. University of Michigan Press, 1986.

Snyder, Gary. *Turtle Island*. New Directions, 1974.

Stevens, Wallace. *The Collected Poems: The Corrected Edition*. Edited by Chris Beyers and John N. Serio. Vintage International. Vintage, 2015.

Students. All statements made by my students are used with permission.

Tate, James, quoted in Dinty W. Moore, *The Mindful Writer*. Wisdom, 2016.

Vygotsky L. S., Michael Cole, Sally Stein, and Allan Sekula. *Mind in Society: The Development of Higher Psychological Processes.* Harvard University Press, 1978.

White, E. B., quoted in John Morreall, *Comic Relief: A Comprehensive Philosophy of Humor.* Wiley-Blackwell, 2009.

Whitman, Walt. *Leaves of Grass: The Complete 1855 and 1891–92 Editions.* Edited by John Hollander. A Library of America Paperback Classic. Library of America, 2011.

Wilde, Oscar. *Lady Windermere's Fan: A Play about a Good Woman.* Methuen, 1917.

Williams, William Carlos. *Paterson.* Edited by Christopher John MacGowan. New Directions Books, 2013.

Williams, William Carlos. *The Collected Poems of William Carlos Williams, Vol. 1: 1909–1939.* Edited by Christopher MacGowan and A. Walton Litz. Reprint edition. New Directions, 1991.

Wordsworth, William. *Selected Poems.* Penguin Classics, 2004.

Yeats, William Butler, and Dorothy Wellesley. *Letters on Poetry from W. B. Yeats to Dorothy Wellesley.* With an introduction by Kathleen Raine. Oxford University Press, 1964.

Yeats, William Butler. *W. B. Yeats: Poems Selected by Seamus Heaney.* Edited by Seamus Heaney. Faber & Faber Ltd., 2001.

Zapruder, Matthew. "Off The Shelf: Finding the Pieces That Turn Writing into Poetry." *Los Angeles Times*, 18 September 2009. www.latimes.com/entertainment/arts/la-caw-off-the-shelf20-2009sep20-story.html.[*]

---

[*]   Note: For missing citations, the original source is unknown.

Index

Ben Berman is the author of *Writing While Parenting, Figuring in the Figure*, and *Strange Borderlands*, all from Able Muse Press in 2022, 2017, 2012 respectively; and *Then Again* (Vine Leaves Press, 2018). He has won the Peace Corps Award for the Best Book of Poetry, has been shortlisted twice for the Massachusetts Book Awards, and has received awards from the Massachusetts Cultural Council, New England Poetry Club, and Somerville Arts Council.

Ben has been teaching for over twenty years and currently teaches creative writing classes at Brookline High School. He lives in the Boston area with his wife and two daughters.

ALSO FROM ABLE MUSE PRESS

Jacob M. Appel, *The Cynic in Extremis: Poems*

William Baer, *Times Square and Other Stories;New Jersey Noir: A Novel;*
New Jersey Noir (Cape May): A Novel; New Jersey Noir (Barnegat Light):A Novel

Lee Harlin Bahan, *A Year of Mourning (Petrarch): Translation*

Melissa Balmain, *Walking in on People (Able Muse Book Award for Poetry)*

Ben Berman, *Strange Borderlands: Poems; Figuring in the Figure: Poems;*
Writing While Parenting: Essays

David Berman, *Progressions of the Mind: Poems*

Lorna Knowles Blake, *Green Hill (Able Muse Book Award for Poetry)*

Michael Cantor, *Life in the Second Circle: Poems*

Catherine Chandler, *Lines of Flight: Poems*

William Conelly, *Uncontested Grounds: Poems*

Maryann Corbett, *Credo for the Checkout Line in Winter: Poems;*
Street View: Poems; In Code: Poems

Will Cordeiro, *Trap Street (Able Muse Book Award for Poetry)*

Brian Culhane, *Remembering Lethe: Poems*

John Philip Drury, *Sea Level Rising: Poems*

Rhina P. Espaillat, *And After All: Poems*

Anna M. Evans, *Under Dark Waters: Surviving the* Titanic: *Poems*

Nicole Caruso Garcia, *Oxblood: Poems*

Stephen Gibson, *Frida Kahlo in Fort Lauderdale: Poems*

D. R. Goodman, *Greed: A Confession: Poems*

Carrie Green, *Studies of Familiar Birds: Poems*

Margaret Ann Griffiths, *Grasshopper: The Poetry of M A Griffiths*

Janis Harrington, *How to Cut a Woman in Half: Poems*

Katie Hartsock, *Bed of Impatiens: Poems; Wolf Trees: Poems*

Elise Hempel, *Second Rain: Poems*

Jan D. Hodge, *Taking Shape: Carmina figurata;*
The Bard & Scheherazade Keep Company: Poems

Ellen Kaufman, *House Music: Poems; Double-Parked, with Tosca: Poems*

Len Krisak, *Say What You Will (Able Muse Book Award for Poetry)*

Emily Leithauser, *The Borrowed World (Able Muse Book Award for Poetry)*

Hailey Leithauser, *Saint Worm: Poems*

Carol Light, *Heaven from Steam: Poems*

Kate Light, *Character Shoes: Poems*

April Lindner, *This Bed Our Bodies Shaped: Poems*

Martin McGovern, *Bad Fame: Poems*

Jeredith Merrin, *Cup: Poems*

Richard Moore, *Selected Poems;*
    The Rule That Liberates: An Expanded Edition: Selected Essays

Richard Newman, *All the Wasted Beauty of the World: Poems*

Alfred Nicol, *Animal Psalms: Poems*

Deirdre O'Connor, *The Cupped Field (Able Muse Book Award for Poetry)*

Frank Osen, *Virtue, Big as Sin (Able Muse Book Award for Poetry)*

Alexander Pepple (Editor), *Able Muse Anthology;*
    Able Muse: A Review of Poetry, Prose & Art (semiannual, winter 2010 on)

James Pollock, *Sailing to Babylon: Poems*

Aaron Poochigian, *The Cosmic Purr: Poems; Manhattanite (Able Muse Book Award for Poetry)*

Tatiana Forero Puerta, *Cleaning the Ghost Room: Poems*

Jennifer Reeser, *Indigenous: Poems; Strong Feather: Poems*

John Ridland, *Sir Gawain and the Green Knight (Anonymous): Translation;*
    Pearl (Anonymous): Translation

Kelly Rowe, *Rise above the River (Able Muse Book Award for Poetry)*

Stephen Scaer, *Pumpkin Chucking: Poems*

Hollis Seamon, *Corporeality: Stories*

Ed Shacklee, *The Blind Loon: A Bestiary*

Carrie Shipers, *Cause for Concern (Able Muse Book Award for Poetry)*

Matthew Buckley Smith, *Dirge for an Imaginary World (Able Muse Book Award for Poetry)*

Susan de Sola, *Frozen Charlotte: Poems*

Barbara Ellen Sorensen, *Compositions of the Dead Playing Flutes: Poems*

Rebecca Starks, *Time Is Always Now: Poems; Fetch, Muse: Poems*

Sally Thomas, *Motherland: Poems*

Paulette Demers Turco (Editor), *The Powow River Poets Anthology II*

Rosemerry Wahtola Trommer, *Naked for Tea: Poems*

Wendy Videlock, *Wise to the West: Poems; Slingshots and Love Plums: Poems;*
    The Dark Gnu and Other Poems; Nevertheless: Poems

Richard Wakefield, *A Vertical Mile: Poems; Terminal Park: Poems*

Gail White, *Asperity Street: Poems*

Chelsea Woodard, *Vellum: Poems*

Rob Wright, *Last Wishes: Poems*

www.ablemusepress.com

CPSIA information can be obtained
at www.ICGtesting.com
Printed in the USA
BVHW030301250223
659179BV00012B/212